JEAN BOWRING'S CASSEROLE COOKBOOK

JEAN BOWRING'S CASSEROLE COOKBOOK

ANGUS AND ROBERTSON
PUBLISHERS

Also by Jean Bowring

CAKE ICING AND DECORATING
JEAN BOWRING'S NEW CAKE DECORATING BOOK
THE JEAN BOWRING COOKBOOK

First published in 1974 by

ANGUS AND ROBERTSON (PUBLISHERS) PTY LTD
102 Glover Street, Cremorne, Sydney
2 Fisher Street, London
159 Boon Keng Road, Singapore
P.O. Box 1072, Makati MCC, Rizal, Philippines
113 Rosslyn Street, West Melbourne
222 East Terrace, Adelaide
1 Little Street, Fortitude Valley, Brisbane

© *Jean Bowring 1974*

National Library of Australia
card number and ISBN 0 207 12733 6

TYPESET AND POSITIVES SUPPLIED BY
FILMSET CENTRE PTY LTD, BRISBANE
PRINTED IN HONG KONG

Acknowledgments

My thanks to the Editor of *Home Beautiful* magazine for the loan of most of the illustrations appearing in my book; and to Kraft Foods Ltd, the Australian Dairy Produce Board, and the Carnation Co Pty Ltd for the loan of other illustrations.

Jean Bowring

Contents

Casseroles—the Food and the Container

Casseroles have come a long way from their humble beginnings when they were not much more than a thrifty solution to the problem of using left-overs. Today a casserole can take its place in a meal as an entrée or as the main course—and be so delicious that you'll hope there will be some of *it* left over!

There's plenty of scope in this branch of cooking: the creative cook can try her hand at interesting food combinations, make a magical pass with seasonings, and sometimes produce a spur-of-the-moment dish so delicious that she will wish she had written down exact quantities of the various ingredients.

But you don't have to experiment when you have a collection of recipes such as this—it has all been done for you. In this book there is a casserole for every occasion from the simplest to the most important, ranging from the meal-in-a-moment dish to the casserole that simmers lazily in the oven requiring no attention until the time comes to serve it. Rarely are casseroles spoilt by overcooking. In many cases they improve by being cooked ahead and then being left to stand overnight for serving at the following day's main meal.

Time and labour can be saved as well, because a casserole may be left in the dish in which it was cooked, then reheated in the same dish. This means no washing up of storage bowls.

On the credit side also there is economy. The cheaper cuts of meat, the coarser fleshed fish, the slightly aged bird or the boiler lend themselves to long, slow gentle cooking, which makes them tender and succulent. Nothing is wasted, for any juices drawn from the meat or vegetables during cooking are captured in the gravy, making the dish rich in flavour.

Choosing Your Casserole Dish

A wide variety of casserole dishes is available today and you would be wise to consider the various materials from which they are made before you purchase one.

THE SIZE

This is important. Too small a casserole could result in the mixture overflowing in the oven, causing waste and work in cleaning up. On the other hand, if the casserole is too large the gravy will reduce and you will find the meat dry.

Be guided by the number of people in the family. It is estimated that a six-cup casserole will serve four or five persons. However, an extra casserole or one twice as big would allow you to make up a double quantity to store in the refrigerator for another meal later in the week, or to freeze if you have a proper freezer (see notes on freezing casseroles).

THE COMPOSITION OF CASSEROLE DISHES

The materials from which casseroles are made range from time-honoured earthenware to modern ceramic glass.

Earthenware was probably one of the first materials used and at present it is enjoying a comeback. Being a good conductor of heat, earthenware is excellent for oven cooking, but it is inclined to be heavy, particularly when the casserole is a large one. It also tends to crack easily, especially if knocked against a hard surface. Earthenware casseroles are not suitable for top-of-the-stove cookery.

Cast iron is another of the casserole materials making a comeback, and like earthenware it is a good conductor of heat. Casseroles made of cast iron can be used for top-of-the-stove cookery, but food should not be left overnight in them. After use they should be thoroughly dried and rubbed with a little oil to prevent them from rusting, then stored. Avoid scouring them after use.

Enamel-finished metal is a durable casserole material provided it is of good quality. Aluminium and cast iron or steel are the metals used. Enamelled aluminium casseroles are the lightest of all. Though cast-iron casseroles with their enamel coating are heavy they pay dividends in the long run if they are of the best quality because they do not chip easily, cooked foods may be stored in them overnight and the vitreous-enamel lining is non-absorbent and hygienic.

2

Copper casseroles—again of the best quality—are practically everlasting. They cook evenly because copper is a good conductor of heat, and they are usually the choice of chefs though they need constant scouring and polishing to keep them gleaming.

Glass oven-proof casseroles are not good conductors of heat but they have several advantages: you can see the food cooking, they are reasonably inexpensive, and the non-porous surface of the glass is hygienic and easy to clean. Should the food stick, all that is necessary is to soak the dish overnight in water. When using this type of casserole care should be taken not to subject it to sudden changes of temperature. Never pour cold water into a hot glass casserole or put it while still hot on a cold or wet surface. Glass casseroles are not suitable for top-of-the-stove cookery.

Ceramic glass, while more expensive than ordinary glass, is just as hygienic and easy to clean and it will withstand sudden changes of temperature from hot to cold or from cold to hot. It is possible to use this type of casserole on the hot plate, but it is not a good conductor of heat and the cooking will be uneven. The best place to use it is in the oven.

Care and Cleaning of Casseroles

Casseroles are easier to clean if lightly greased before the food is placed in them to cook. Most stains come off after overnight soaking in cold water. If enamel or ceramic casseroles become stained add a little household bleach to the soaking water.

Freezing Casseroles

If there is a low-freezing compartment in your domestic refrigerator, or you have a separate deep-freeze unit, casseroles can play an important part in menu planning and save time and work. It is easy to double the quantities when cooking a casserole, then use half for the immediate meal and freeze the remainder for use later on when you have a particularly busy day or have unexpected guests, or when you wish to take advantage of a good meat bargain or of vegetables in glut supply.

Whether you are following a simple recipe or a gourmet recipe remember to select ingredients of the best quality if the dish is to be frozen for later use. Freezing does not improve foods, but the original flavour, colour and nutritive value will be retained if you use the proper wrapping, packaging or container. Whatever type is used, it must be moisture-proof. In the long run it is more economical to buy packaging materials that can be re-used: polythene bags, aluminium foil containers, freezer jars and plastic or waxed lined freezer containers are a few examples of re-usable materials. Don't use waxed paper, bread-wraps, paper bags or cellophane—none of these are moisture-proof.

3

Glass jars with wide necks and screw-top lids are excellent for freezer use but they must be carefully handled, especially when frozen, or they will break.

The following hints will help you if you are thinking of preparing and cooking a casserole for freezing:

1. Don't overcook the casserole: remember that the food will be subjected to more cooking when it is reheated.

2. Salt or season lightly: you can always add a little more when the casserole is being reheated before it is served.

3. Cool the cooked food as quickly as possible. The easiest and quickest way to do this is to place the casserole of hot food in a bowl or sink containing iced water. This arrests the cooking action (which normally goes on to a certain extent while a casserole is cooling) and it also retards or prevents the growth of bacteria and reduces the possibility of the food when thawed and reheated having that "left-over" taste.

4. Label, date and identify each package before placing it in the freezer, expecially if foil-wrapped.

5. If you use jars or cartons allow a little room for the expansion of the liquid in the casserole.

STORAGE PERIODS IN DEEP FREEZERS

The storage life of cooked foods is much shorter than that of uncooked foods. Storage for too long results in a change in both the colour and the texture of the food.

Meat casseroles in a deep freezer should be used within three to six months.

Pasta and cheese casseroles should be used within three months.

Casseroles containing shellfish should not be stored longer than one or two months, because the flesh of the shellfish tends to toughen during long storage.

Boiled potatoes are inclined to become watery when frozen, and if potatoes are included in the ingredients I suggest omitting them from a casserole that is to be frozen or adding them when the casserole is being reheated (at the end of the storage period).

Avoid putting hard-boiled eggs in casseroles that are to be frozen: egg white becomes leathery when frozen.

TO PREPARE FROZEN CASSEROLES FOR SERVING

To reheat a casserole that has been frozen either place the frozen food back in the casserole in which it was cooked and reheat in a hot oven, or place it in a saucepan over low heat. The second method needs special care, for the mixture will need stirring during the reheating period and this could result in the vegetables and meat breaking up and the texture of the dish being spoilt.

Creamed dishes such as mornays are usually reheated by being placed in the top of a double saucepan, but they can also be reheated successfully in a slow to moderate oven.

Metric Conversion in Ingredient Measures

The list of ingredients in each recipe in this book includes both Imperial measures and their nearest metric equivalents or recommended alternatives. For canned and most packaged goods bought at supermarkets and grocery shops the metric equivalents are to the nearest whole number, as in column 2 of the following table; for products bought from greengrocers', butchers' and fish shops and bulk stores it is recommended that the conversion should be rounded on the basis of 500 g as the alternative to 1 lb, as in column 3 of the table.

CUP AND SPOON MEASUREMENTS

Cup measurements for all recipes in this book are based on the 8-fluid-ounce cup, which equals, in rounded figures, 227 millilitres. The metric cup, when available, will contain 250 millilitres; if this is used the quantity measured should be reduced by about 10 per cent.

Spoon measurements (20 ml tablespoon and 5 ml teaspoon) remain the same.

Imperial ounce (oz)	Metric conversion to nearest whole number gram (g)	Recommended metric equivalent gram (g)
1	28	30
2	57	60
3	85	90
$3\frac{1}{2}$	99	
4	113	125
5	142	
6	170	
$6\frac{1}{2}$	184	
$6\frac{3}{4}$	191	
7	198	
$7\frac{1}{2}$	213	
$7\frac{3}{4}$	220	
8	227	250
9	255	
10	283	
$10\frac{1}{2}$	298	
11	312	
12	340	375
13	369	
14	397	
15	425	
$15\frac{1}{4}$	432	
$15\frac{1}{2}$	439	
16	454	500

Barbecued Hamburger Casserole

1½ lb or 750 g finely minced steak
⅔ cup soft white breadcrumbs
2 tablespoons chopped onion
2 tablespoons prepared
   horseradish (optional)
1½ teaspoons salt
¼ teaspoon pepper
⅔ cup unsweetened canned milk
For the sauce
3 tablespoons chopped onion
1 green pepper seeded and chopped
15½ oz or 439 g can tomato soup
2 tablespoons brown sugar
juice of 1 medium lemon
2 tablespoons Worcester sauce
2 tablespoons corn relish

Combine the ingredients for the hamburgers in the order given and mix lightly but thoroughly. Form into patties, using a little seasoned flour. Heat approximately 2 tablespoons of oil or melted butter in a pan and cook the hamburgers until a golden brown on both sides. Drain on paper and place in a lightly greased casserole.

In the same pan sauté the onion and green pepper for about 3 minutes. Pour off any surplus oil and add the remaining sauce ingredients. Stir until boiling, then pour over the hamburgers in the casserole. Cover and cook in a moderate oven (350° F, 180° C) for approximately 45 minutes.

Beef Burgundy

3 rashers of bacon, diced
2 lb or 1 kg good stewing steak
   cut into 1-inch cubes
1 tablespoon brandy
1 tablespoon butter
1 clove of garlic, crushed
1 lb or 500 g sliced mushrooms
6 small white onions
$\frac{1}{4}$ cup butter
$\frac{1}{2}$ cup plain flour
2 cups canned beef consommé
$\frac{3}{4}$ cup burgundy
1 bay-leaf
1 tablespoon chopped parsley
$\frac{1}{4}$ teaspoon salt
$\frac{1}{2}$ teaspoon thyme
dash of pepper
2 carrots sliced

Brown the diced bacon in a heavy-based pan then lift out and set aside. In the bacon fat brown the cubed beef, stirring frequently. Warm the brandy, ignite and pour over the beef.

Add 1 tablespoon of butter to the pan and sauté the garlic, mushrooms and onions for about 5 minutes. Remove and set aside.

Add the $\frac{1}{4}$ cup butter to the pan and stir in the flour. Keep stirring until brown, then add the beef consommé and the burgundy and stir until the mixture boils and slightly thickens. Add the reserved bacon, the mushroom mixture, bay-leaf, parsley, salt, thyme, pepper and carrots. Bring to the boil and pour over the meat in the casserole. Cover and cook in a moderate oven (350° F, 180° C) for about 2 hours or until the meat is tender.

Beef Burgundy

Beef Casserole 1

2 lb or 1 kg round steak
2 tablespoons plain flour
3 tablespoons bacon fat or butter
1 teaspoon salt
1¾ cups stock, or water and
   2 teaspoons instant stock
1 tablespoon vinegar
1 tablespoon Worcester sauce
1 tablespoon tomato sauce
1 bay-leaf
6 small or 3 medium onions
6 small or 2 large carrots
1 cup sliced mushrooms

Cut the steak into cubes and toss in the plain flour. Heat the bacon fat or butter in a heavy-based pan and brown the steak lightly. Lift out with a slotted spoon and place in the casserole.

To the fat left in the pan add the flour left over from coating the meat, and the salt. Stir until brown and then add the water or stock, the vinegar and sauces. Stir until boiling.

Pour this gravy into the casserole and add the bay-leaf. Cover and cook in a moderate oven (350° F, 180° C) for about half an hour then add the vegetables and continue to cook for a further 1½ hours or until both the meat and the vegetables are tender.

Beef Casserole 2

2 tablespoons oil
2 lb or 1 kg lean beef cut into
   cubes
2 tablespoons plain flour
1 cup red wine
1 cup water
1 clove of garlic crushed
1 bay-leaf
½ teaspoon thyme
3 sprigs parsley
1 teaspoon salt
¼ teaspoon pepper
6 baby carrots
6 small onions peeled
6 small potatoes peeled
2 medium parsnips peeled
2 cups cooked green peas

Heat the oil in a pan and brown the beef cubes. Sprinkle in the flour and cook until lightly browned, then add the wine, water, crushed garlic, bay-leaf, thyme, parsley, salt and pepper. Stir until boiling then transfer to a casserole.

Cover and cook in a moderate oven (350° F, 180° C) for about 1½ hours, then add the prepared vegetables except for the peas. You may have to cut the potatoes and parsnips, if they are large, to make them uniform in size. Cover and cook for another 45 minutes. Add the peas just before serving.

Beef Casserole Italienne

1 tablespoon salad oil
2 lb or 1 kg oyster blade steak
  cut into cubes
$\frac{1}{2}$ lb or 250 g fresh mushrooms
  sliced
$15\frac{1}{2}$ oz or 439 g can whole
  tomatoes
3 large carrots cut into thick
  slices
3 small onions peeled and sliced
$\frac{1}{2}$ teaspoon oregano
$\frac{1}{2}$ teaspoon basil
2 teaspoons salt
good pinch of pepper
1 clove of garlic crushed
2 teaspoons cornflour
3 tablespoons sour or fresh cream

Heat the oil in a large pan and brown the meat on all sides. Push the meat to one side of the pan and sauté the mushrooms. Add the tomatoes (including the juice), carrots, onions, oregano, basil, salt, pepper and garlic. Put in a casserole, cover and cook in a moderate oven (350° F, 180° C) for about 2 hours or until the meat is tender.

Blend the cornflour with the cream, add to the contents of the casserole, cover and replace in the oven to cook for a further 15 minutes.

Beef Casserole Italienne

Beef en Daube

3 rashers of bacon
2 lb or 1 kg stewing steak
$\frac{1}{2}$ cup beef stock
1 cup dry red wine
1 teaspoon salt
$\frac{1}{4}$ teaspoon thyme
2 cloves of garlic crushed
$\frac{1}{2}$ cup minced onion
2 strips orange rind
1 tablespoon cornflour
1 tablespoon brandy
12 whole small onions, or 3
 medium onions cut into four
$\frac{3}{4}$ lb or 375 g fresh mushrooms
1$\frac{1}{2}$ tablespoons butter
1 teaspoon sugar
1 packet frozen peas thawed

Remove the rind and cut the bacon into 1-inch pieces. Sauté until crisp in a heavy-based pan. Lift out and set aside. Pour off all but 2 tablespoons of fat, dice the meat, add it to the pan and brown on all sides. Add the stock, wine, salt, thyme, garlic, onion and orange rind.

Place the mixture in a casserole, cover and cook in a moderate oven for 1 to 1$\frac{1}{4}$ hours. Blend the cornflour with the brandy, stir into the casserole then continue to bake.

Peel the onions and cook in boiling salted water until barely tender, about 15 minutes. Drain. Cut the stems from the mushrooms, slice them and sauté with the whole caps of the mushrooms in a tablespoon of butter until barely tender. Add to the casserole.

In the same pan sauté the onions in the remaining butter until lightly browned, sprinkle with sugar and heat until glazed lightly. Add to the casserole. Now add the thawed peas and bacon, return the casserole to the oven for a further 10 minutes or until thoroughly heated.

Beef Goulash with Gherkins

1 tablespoon butter
2 medium onions peeled and
 chopped
2 teaspoons paprika
2 lb or 1 kg round steak
1$\frac{1}{2}$ tablespoons seasoned plain
 flour
4 tablespoons red wine
1 cup beef stock, or water and
 1 soup cube
$\frac{1}{3}$ teaspoon salt
freshly ground black pepper
6 gherkins cut into julienne strips

Heat the butter in a heavy-based pan and add the onions. Cook, stirring occasionally, until they are lightly coloured. Remove from the heat and add the paprika. Stir to coat the onions. Turn the mixture into a casserole.

Cut the steak into 1-inch cubes and toss in the seasoned flour. Using the same pan, and adding a little more butter, lightly fry the meat until it changes colour. Add the wine, stock, salt and a little pepper and bring to the boil. Transfer to a casserole. Cover and cook in a moderate oven (350° F, 180° C) for about 2 hours or until the meat is tender. Add the gherkins and return the casserole to the oven to cook for about 10 minutes before serving.

Beef Hot-Pot Casserole

2 lb or 1 kg blade or topside
    steak
2 tablespoons butter
2 teaspoons oil
1 cup chopped onions
2 tablespoons plain flour
1 clove of garlic crushed
½ teaspoon thyme
1 teaspoon salt
¼ teaspoon pepper
1½ cups water
3 tablespoons tomato paste
1 medium green pepper
⅔ cup unsweetened canned milk
1 tablespoon lemon juice
tomato, black olives and parsley
    to garnish

Remove any excess fat from the meat before cutting into 1-inch cubes. Brown the meat a few pieces at a time in the heated butter and oil, using a shallow pan. Lift out as the pieces brown and place in a casserole.

Sauté the onions in the butter and oil left in the pan (add a little more butter if required), then stir in the flour and the seasonings. Cook until lightly browned, add the water and tomato paste and stir until the mixture boils and thickens. Pour over the meat in the casserole, cover and cook in a moderate oven for about 1½ hours or until almost tender.

Cut the pepper into thin strips and blanch in boiling water. Drain and add to the casserole. Cook for a further 15 minutes. Just before serving add the milk and lemon juice. Reheat without boiling, adjust the seasonings and serve with a black olive, tomato and parsley garnish and accompany with cooked noodles, freshly boiled rice or fried potato balls.

Beef Bourguignonne

4 rashers of bacon
3 lb or 1.5 kg round or buttock
    steak
seasoned plain flour
1 tablespoon oil
1 tablespoon butter
salt and pepper
4 tablespoons warmed brandy
2 medium carrots cut into thick
    slices
½ bunch shallots
1 large onion peeled and sliced
1 clove of garlic crushed
1 bouquet garni (1 large bay-

Remove the rind and cut the bacon into 1-inch pieces. Fry until the fat is clear, then lift out with a slotted spoon. Cut the steak into cubes and roll them in seasoned flour.

To the bacon fat in the pan add the butter and oil and fry the meat until it is brown on all sides. Season it well with salt and pepper and then pour over the warmed brandy. Ignite it and let the flames die. Turn the mixture in the pan into a casserole.

Sauté the carrots in the pan, adding more butter and oil if necessary, then add the shallot, onion, garlic and bouquet garni. Sauté briefly, then add the burgundy and stock and bring to

leaf, 1 sprig thyme, 6 sprigs
parsley and 2 pieces celery tops
tied together with white twine)
1½ cups burgundy
1½ cups stock
12 tiny white onions
½ lb or 250 g button mushrooms
a little sugar
a little lemon juice
chopped parsley to garnish

the boil. Pour this liquid over the meat in the casserole and add the bacon. Cover and cook in a moderate oven (350° F, 180° C) for about 2 hours.

Brown the onions in a little butter in a pan, add a little sugar and some burgundy and simmer until the onions are tender. Add to the casserole. In the same pan sauté the mushrooms in butter and add a little lemon juice. Remove the bouquet garni from the casserole and add the mushrooms. Replace in the oven to reheat thoroughly, then serve with a generous sprinkling of chopped parsley.

Beef Maison

1 whole eye of beef fillet
2 teaspoons butter
1 teaspoon made mustard
¼ teaspoon ground ginger
freshly ground black pepper
salt
½ cup red wine
½ lb or 250 g fresh mushrooms
   sautéed

Trim any fat from the fillet and place it in a lightly greased casserole. Brush with the melted butter and then with the mustard. Sprinkle over the ginger, pepper and salt. Pour over the wine. Cover and cook in a moderate oven (350° F, 180° C) for 30 to 45 minutes. Remove the lid and bake for a further 15 minutes.

To serve, slice the fillet into thick slices and overlap them on a hot serving dish, or replace in the casserole. Serve with the juices in the casserole and accompany with sautéed mushrooms.

The cooking time will depend on the taste of the person for whom it is being prepared. The above times produce a rare steak.

Beef Olive Casserole

2 lb or 1 kg buttock, round or
   topside steak
¼ cup soy sauce
¼ cup sherry
¼ cup tarragon vinegar
½ teaspoon black pepper
⅔ cup chopped onion

Cut the meat into thin slices and pound into neat oblong pieces with a meat mallet. Combine the soy sauce, sherry, tarragon vinegar and pepper and pour over the steak. Marinade for 2 hours, turning occasionally.

Sauté the onion and the green pepper in the butter until tender. Add the celery, parsley, salt

$\frac{2}{3}$ cup chopped green pepper
$1\frac{1}{2}$ tablespoons butter
$\frac{1}{3}$ cup chopped celery
$\frac{1}{4}$ cup chopped parsley
$\frac{1}{2}$ teaspoon salt
pinch of pepper
2 rounded tablespoons soft
   white breadcrumbs
1 level tablespoon plain flour
1 tablespoon cold water

and pepper and cook for 5 minutes longer. Stir in the breadcrumbs and allow to cool.

Remove the steak from the marinade and drain it well. Arrange the vegetable mixture on the pieces of steak and roll up firmly, securing each with a wooden cocktail pick or with fine string. Brown them in a pan in a little hot fat, drain and place in a casserole. Pour the marinade into the pan and thicken with the blended flour. Stir until boiling, then pour over the beef rolls. Cover and cook in a moderate oven (350° F, 180° C) for about $1\frac{1}{2}$ hours or until tender.

Beef Olive Casserole

Beef Olives with Savoury Sauce

1 lb or 500 g round steak
½ lb or 250 g sausage meat
2 tablespoons chopped onions
1 clove of garlic (optional)
   crushed
seasoned plain flour
2 tablespoons butter or oil
1 cup water
1 beef soup cube
1 tablespoon plain flour
1 teaspoon Worcester sauce
1 tablespoon tomato sauce
½ teaspoon brown sugar

Trim the steak, removing any excess fat, then cut it into 2-inch squares. Using a meat mallet, pound the meat until thin, being careful not to break the fibres.

Mix the sausage meat with the onion and crushed garlic. Place a small amount on each piece of meat and roll up, securing with wooden cocktail picks. Roll the meat in seasoned flour, then fry in the hot butter or oil until brown all over. Lift out with a slotted spoon, drain on paper and place in a casserole.

Pour away all but 1 tablespoon of oil or butter, add the flour, stir until smooth, then cook for a few minutes to brown. Add the water, soup cube, Worcester sauce, tomato sauce and brown sugar and stir until boiling. Pour over the meat, cover and cook in a moderate oven (350° F, 180° C) for about 1 hour or until the meat is tender. Remove the cocktail picks before serving.

Beef Paupiettes with Mushrooms

2½ lb or 1.25 kg piece topside
3 tablespoons butter
1 onion peeled and cut into rings
15½ oz or 439 g can tomato purée
¾ cup claret
1 tablespoon sugar
8 oz or 250 g small cultivated
   mushrooms
For the stuffing
2 cups soft white breadcrumbs
1 tablespoon chopped parsley
¼ teaspoon oregano
1 teaspoon grated lemon rind
2 rashers of bacon finely chopped
salt and pepper
1 egg

Cut the beef into thin slices. Flatten each piece with a meat mallet and cut into bite-size squares. Combine the ingredients for the stuffing and spread some on each square. Roll up and secure with wooden cocktail picks.

Melt 2 tablespoons of the butter in a pan, sauté the onion rings for a few minutes, then add the paupiettes and brown them on all sides. Add the tomato purée, claret and sugar. Place in a lightly greased casserole, cover and cook in a moderate oven (350° F, 180° C) for 1 hour. Remove from the casserole and strain over a bowl. Remove the wooden picks from the paupiettes, then return them to the casserole. Cover and keep warm.

Heat the remaining butter in a pan, add the mushrooms and sauté over high heat for 2 or 3 minutes, shaking the pan occasionally. Pour in the sauce, boil until it is a good consistency, then pour it over the paupiettes in the casserole. Cover and reheat in a moderate oven (temperature as above). Serve with buttered noodles, braised whole onions and carrots.

Beef Rouladen with Mushroom Sauce

3 lb or 1.5 kg round steak
seasoned plain flour
3 tablespoons butter
1 cup dry white wine
1 cup beef stock, or water and
   1 beef soup cube
1 teaspoon salt
freshly ground black pepper
1½ slightly rounded tablespoons
   cornflour
1½ tablespoons cold water
½ lb or 250 g mushrooms
chopped parsley
For the filling
2 medium onions finely chopped
¼ lb or 125 g mushrooms finely
   chopped
1 tablespoon butter
½ cup to 1 cup chopped ham
¼ cup grated Parmesan cheese

First make the filling: sauté the onions and mushrooms in 1 tablespoon of the butter until both are soft, then add the ham and cheese. Mix well and allow to cool.

Remove any excess fat and pound the meat until very thin. Cut it into pieces about 3 by 5 inches. You should have between 20 and 24 pieces. Place a heaped tablespoon of the filling on each piece of meat, fold in the sides then roll the steak up tightly. Secure each roll with wooden cocktail picks and coat lightly with seasoned flour.

Heat the remaining 2 tablespoons of butter in a pan and fry the rolls until brown on all sides. Lift out and place in a casserole.

To the pan add the wine and stock with salt and pepper to taste, and stir until boiling. Pour over the rolls in the casserole. Cover and cook in a moderate oven (350° F, 180° C) for about 40 minutes. Take the casserole from the oven and lift out the rolls with a slotted spoon. Remove the wooden cocktail picks.

While the casserole is out of the oven blend the cornflour with the cold water and stir into the beef casserole. Replace the rolls, cover and replace in the oven.

Sauté the mushrooms in the butter until they begin to soften, then add to the casserole and continue to cook for another 25 to 30 minutes or until the rolls are tender. Serve topped with chopped parsley and accompanied with buttered rice.

Beefball Stroganoff

1½ lb or 750 g finely minced steak
⅓ cup dry breadcrumbs
¼ cup chopped onion
1 teaspoon salt
¼ teaspoon pepper
1 egg
1 teaspoon Worcester sauce
2 tablespoons butter for frying
For the sauce
¼ cup chopped onion
10½ oz or 298 g can cream of
  mushroom soup
½ soup can water or stock
1 to 2 tablespoons fresh or
  cultured sour cream

Combine the steak, breadcrumbs, onion, salt and pepper. Beat the egg and add the Worcester sauce, and add enough to bind the meat mixture together. Take spoonfuls and shape into 18 balls each about 2 inches in diameter. A little seasoned flour may be used for shaping. Brown the meatballs in the hot butter, lift out and place in a casserole.

Add the chopped onion for the sauce to the same pan and sauté until soft but not brown. Add the undiluted soup and the stock and stir until boiling. Pour over the beefballs in the casserole. Cover and cook in a moderate oven (350° F, 180° C) for about 40 minutes. Stir in the cream and reheat. If liked, serve the beefballs over freshly cooked rice, with a chopped parsley garnish.

Bitochki

1 lb or 500 g finely minced steak
½ cup soft white breadcrumbs
1 teaspoon salt
1 tablespoon chopped onion
1 beaten egg to mix
butter or fat for frying
15½ oz or 439 g can cream of
  mushroom soup
½ soup can water

Combine the minced steak with the breadcrumbs, salt, chopped onion and enough beaten egg to mix. Blend lightly. Take spoonfuls and make into balls, then roll the balls in more breadcrumbs.

Heat a little butter or fat in a pan and fry the meatballs until lightly browned all over. Drain on paper, place in a lightly greased casserole and add the soup and water. Cover and cook for about 30 minutes in a moderate oven (350° F, 180° C). Thin down with a little milk if you find the sauce too thick.

Bobotie

2 tablespoons butter
2 medium onions peeled and
  sliced
2 lb or 1 kg minced steak
1 egg

Melt the butter in a pan and fry the onions until golden. Add the minced steak and cook, stirring constantly, until it changes colour.

In a large bowl combine the egg, milk and bread cubes, mixing well. Stir in the apricots,

Bobotie

¼ cup milk
2 slices bread cubed
¼ cup dried apricots minced
¼ cup raisins
12 blanched almonds chopped
    (or 2 tablespoons salted
    peanuts)
2 tablespoons sugar
1 tablespoon curry powder
2 tablespoons lemon juice
2 teaspoons salt
¼ teaspoon pepper
3 bay-leaves
For the topping
1 egg
¾ cup milk
¼ teaspoon turmeric

raisins, nuts, sugar, curry powder, lemon juice, salt and pepper. Add to the meat mixture, mixing lightly. Turn into a lightly greased casserole. Press the bay-leaves into the mixture and bake uncovered in a moderate oven (350° F, 180° C) for 30 minutes.

For the topping combine the beaten egg with the milk and turmeric. Remove the casserole from the oven, discard the bay-leaves and pour the topping over the mixture in the casserole. Return it to the oven and bake uncovered for another 20 minutes or until the topping has set. Serve with freshly boiled rice and chutney.

Beef a la Mode

2 lb or 1 kg topside or round
  steak
plain flour
4 rashers of bacon
1 tablespoon oil
1 tablespoon butter
salt
freshly ground black pepper
3 tablespoons cognac warmed
1 large carrot scraped and sliced
1 leek sliced
3 shallots peeled and chopped
1 onion peeled and chopped
1 clove of garlic crushed
1 bouquet garni
1 cup red burgundy
1 cup water or stock
2 teaspoons plain flour
2 teaspoons butter
8 button onions
12 button mushrooms
sugar
lemon juice
chopped parsley to garnish

Remove any fat and cut the steak into fairly large cubes. Toss in flour. Remove the rind and fry the bacon until the fat is clear. Lift out and place in a casserole.

Add the oil and butter to the pan and brown the steak on all sides, sprinkling it with salt and pepper. Sprinkle over the warmed cognac, ignite it, let the flames die down and transfer the meat to the casserole.

Prepare the carrots, leek, shallots and onion and put them into the fat remaining in the pan. Cook, stirring lightly, until they begin to brown (you may need a little more oil and butter to prevent them from sticking to the pan). Add the crushed garlic with the vegetables and the bouquet garni to the casserole.

Add all but 4 tablespoons of the wine, then the water or stock, and cover and cook in a moderate oven (350° F, 180° C) for 1½ to 2 hours.

Remove any fat from the surface of the casserole and gradually stir in the butter and flour which have been creamed together. Replace the lid and return the casserole to the oven to cook for another hour.

Brown the button onions (or use chopped shallots) in a little butter in a pan and sprinkle with the sugar. Add the reserved 4 tablespoons of burgundy, cover and cook until the onions are tender. Sauté the mushrooms in a little butter and add a good squeeze of lemon juice. Keep warm. When the meat is tender remove the bouquet garni, taste and add more salt if necessary, then add the sautéed onions and mushrooms. Sprinkle liberally with chopped parsley before serving.

Chili con Carne

2 cups brown kidney beans
½ teaspoon salt
2 tablespoons oil or lard

Soak the kidney beans overnight. Next morning drain them, place in a saucepan with cold water and the salt and bring to the boil. Cook for 40

2 medium onions

1½ lb or 750 g stewing steak

about 1½ tablespoons seasoned plain flour

3 fresh tomatoes peeled and quartered

1 green pepper seeded and chopped

½ cup boiling water

1 clove of garlic peeled and crushed

1 or more tablespoons of chili powder

½ teaspoon dry mustard

2 teaspoons red or white wine

1 teaspoon brown sugar

minutes or until tender. Drain well.

Heat the oil in a pan, stir in the thinly sliced onions and cook until a golden brown. Lift out and place in a casserole. Cut the meat into ½-inch cubes, roll in the seasoned flour and fry in the same pan until brown on all sides. Place in the casserole.

In the same pan place the tomato quarters, chopped green pepper and boiling water. As the mixture comes back to the boil add the garlic, chili powder and mustard. Pour over the onions and meat in the casserole. Cover and cook in a moderate oven for about 45 minutes.

Add the kidney beans, cover and cook for a further 30 minutes, then add the wine and brown sugar, cover again and continue cooking until the meat is tender but not ragged. Taste and add more salt if necessary before serving.

Chip Puff Stroganoff

1 tablespoon butter

½ cup chopped onion

1½ lb or 750 g finely minced steak

2 tablespoons plain flour

¾ cup water

1 beef soup cube

½ teaspoon salt

dash of pepper

10½ oz or 298 g can cream of mushroom soup

1 cup cultured sour cream

For the chip puffs

¾ cup water

½ teaspoon salt

1 tablespoon butter

¾ cup milk

1 packet instant mashed potato

8 one-inch cubes of cheese

1 to 1½ cups crumbled potato crisps

Heat the butter in a saucepan and cook the onion until soft. Add the meat and cook, stirring constantly, until it changes colour. Add the flour and mix well. Now stir in the water, the crumbled soup cube, and the salt and pepper. Cook until the mixture has thickened slightly, then add the soup and the sour cream. Bring to the boil and pour into a lightly greased casserole.

To make the puffs combine the water, salt and butter and bring to the boil, remove from the heat and add the milk, then stir into the instant mashed potato, using a fork to keep the potato light. Take portions, shape into 8 balls and insert a cheese cube in the middle of each. Roll the balls in the crushed potato crisps.

Place the puffs on top of the meat in the casserole and cook uncovered in a hot oven (425° F, 220° C) for about 25 minutes or until the puffs are a golden brown.

Curried Beef Casserole

3 lb or 1.5 kg round or chuck
  steak
1 teaspoon salt
2 tablespoons or more of curry
  powder
1 tablespoon butter
1 tablespoon oil
2 small onions peeled and sliced
1 clove of garlic chopped
1 slightly rounded tablespoon
  plain flour
1½ cups water
1 or 2 soup cubes
1 bay-leaf
1 teaspoon sugar
1 cooking apple peeled and diced
½ cup sultanas (optional)
1 large banana peeled and sliced
juice of ½ lemon
1 large tomato peeled and
  chopped

This curry is improved by being made the day before it is needed, then reheated slowly in a moderate oven.

Remove any fat and cut the steak into ¼-inch cubes. Put the meat into a bowl with the salt and curry powder and mix well.

Heat the butter and oil in a heavy-based pan or flame-proof casserole and fry the onion and garlic. Lift out, add more butter if necessary and fry the meat until brown. Sprinkle the flour in, then add the water and soup cube and stir until the mixture boils and thickens. Turn into a large, lightly greased casserole.

Add the bay-leaf, sugar, apple, sultana, banana, lemon juice, tomato, cooked onion and garlic. Cover and cook in a moderate oven (350° F, 180° C) for at least 2 hours. Serve with freshly boiled rice.

Devilled Steak

1½ lb or 750 g good stewing steak
2 tablespoons seasoned plain
  flour
1 large onion peeled and sliced
1 clove of garlic crushed or
  minced
½ teaspoon dry mustard
¼ teaspoon thyme
salt and pepper
1 teaspoon brown sugar
1 tablespoon vinegar
1 tablespoon Worcester sauce
2 tablespoons tomato sauce
1 bay-leaf
1 lb or 500 g potatoes peeled and
  thickly sliced
chopped parsley to garnish

Trim any excess fat from the steak before cutting it into 1-inch cubes. Toss in the seasoned flour. Place alternate layers of sliced onion, garlic, and cubed steak in a greased casserole.

Combine the mustard, thyme, salt and pepper to taste, and the brown sugar with the vinegar, Worcester and tomato sauce and enough cold water to make up to 1¼ cups. Pour this mixture over the meat and vegetables, then add the bay-leaf. Cover and allow to stand for about 2 hours. Now top with the thickly sliced potatoes. Cover and cook in a moderate oven (350° F, 180° C) for 2 hours or until both the meat and vegetables are tender. Top with chopped parsley and serve the steak directly from the casserole.

Family Beef Casserole

2 lb or 1.5 kg round or good
   stewing steak
2 tablespoons seasoned plain
   flour
2 tablespoons oil or butter
1½ cups water
2 beef soup cubes or 2 teaspoons
   instant mushroom stock
¼ cup tomato sauce
1 tablespoon Worcester sauce
1 clove of garlic crushed
1 bay-leaf
1 teaspoon salt
¼ teaspoon pepper
4 small whole peeled onions
4 small carrots scraped
2 small parsnips scraped
4 small potatoes peeled
2 tablespoons chopped parsley
   to garnish

Cut the meat into 1-inch cubes and coat with seasoned flour. Heat the oil or butter in a shallow pan and brown the meat on all sides. Lift out and place in a casserole.

Add any remaining flour to the pan and stir until it is brown, then add the water, crumbled soup cubes, tomato sauce and Worcester sauce, garlic, bay-leaf, salt and pepper. Stir until boiling, then pour over the meat. Cover and cook in a moderate oven (350° F, 180° C) for about 1½ hours.

Prepare the vegetables, cutting them into uniform sized pieces. Add to the casserole, cover, replace in the oven and cook for a further 45 minutes or until both the meat and the vegetables are tender. Remove the bay-leaf and serve the casserole sprinkled with chopped parsley.

Fillet of Beef Burgundy

1 whole beef fillet (about 2½ to
   3 lb or 2 kg)
1 teaspoon salt
dash of black pepper
½ teaspoon rosemary
5 or 6 rashers of bacon
½ cup burgundy
12 or 16 large mushrooms
6 shallots
¼ cup butter
For the Bordelaise sauce
¼ cup butter
2 shallots finely chopped
2 cloves of garlic peeled and
   crushed
2 slices onion

Trim any fat from the fillet of beef and sprinkle with the salt, pepper and rosemary. Tuck the narrow end of the fillet under to make the meat a uniform thickness. Skewer into shape. Place in a casserole and arrange the bacon rashers on top. Bake uncovered at 450° F (230° C) for 15 or 20 minutes. Reduce the oven temperature to 350° F (180° C) and pour the burgundy over the meat. Cover and cook for about 35 minutes, basting occasionally with the wine and drippings in the casserole.

Meanwhile wash and slice the mushrooms and chop the shallots. Melt the butter in a frying pan and sauté the shallots and mushrooms until tender. Season to taste with salt and pepper. Spoon over the fillet, cover and keep hot in a

2 slices carrot
2 sprigs parsley
10 whole black peppercorns
2 whole cloves
2 bay-leaves
1½ tablespoons plain flour
1¼ cups beef consommé
1 crumbled beef soup cube
1 cup burgundy
¼ teaspoon salt
dash of pepper
1 tablespoon finely chopped
  parsley

moderate oven while you make the sauce, which is served separately.

To make the sauce, first melt the butter in a heavy-based pan and sauté the shallots, garlic, onion, carrot, parsley sprigs, peppercorns, cloves and bay-leaves for about 5 minutes. Stir in the flour till smooth, then cook until lightly browned.

Remove from the heat and add the beef consommé, crumbled soup cube and three-quarters of the cup of burgundy.

Return the pan to the heat and cook, stirring until boiling. Reduce the heat and simmer uncovered for 10 minutes, stirring occasionally. Strain the sauce, discarding the vegetable and spices. Return the sauce to the heat, add the salt, pepper, chopped parsley and the rest of the burgundy. Reheat without boiling. Taste and add more salt if required.

Gourmet Casserole

4 rashers of streaky bacon
2 medium onions peeled and
  chopped
1 clove of garlic peeled and
  crushed
1 large carrot scraped and sliced
2 lb or 1.5 kg round steak cut
  into cubes
2 tablespoons plain flour
1½ teaspoons salt
freshly ground black pepper
1 cup stock, or water and 1 soup
  cube
½ cup red wine
1 large green pepper seeded and
  chopped

Remove the rind and cut the bacon into 1-inch pieces. Fry until the fat is clear, then lift out with a slotted spoon and place in a casserole. Pour off all but 1 tablespoon of bacon fat, add the onions and cook until soft but not brown. Now add the carrots and the garlic and cook for a further 5 minutes. Remove the vegetables and place in a casserole.

Add a little more bacon fat or butter to the pan and add the meat which has been tossed in the flour, salt and pepper. Cook, stirring constantly, until it changes colour, then lift out with a slotted spoon and place in the casserole.

Add the stock and wine to the pan and stir until boiling. Pour over the meat and vegetables in the casserole. Cover and cook in a moderate oven (350° F, 180° C) for 1½ hours. Add the green pepper, cover and continue to cook for a further hour or until the meat is tender.

Pickled walnuts or mushrooms may be used in place of the green pepper. Add 6 pickled walnuts, cut into slices, or 1 cup sliced mushrooms.

Marinated Beef Casserole

2 lb or 1.5 kg round or buttock
  steak
½ cup vinegar
½ cup water
1 clove of garlic crushed
2 teaspoons salt
½ cup sliced onion
1 bay-leaf
12 peppercorns
1 teaspoon sugar
2 tablespoons butter
2 slightly rounded tablespoons
  plain flour
6 tiny white onions or 1 large
  onion cut into 8 wedges
4 small carrots scraped and sliced
parsley to garnish

Trim the steak of any excess fat and cut into cubes. Combine the vinegar and water and bring to the boil, add the garlic, salt, onions, bay-leaf, peppercorns and sugar. Pour this marinade over the cubed meat and let stand overnight. Drain the steak well and reserve ½ cup of the strained marinade.

Heat the butter in a heavy-based pan and brown the meat on all sides. Lift out and place in a casserole. Add the flour to the butter remaining in the pan and stir until brown. Add 1½ cups of water and the reserved ½ cup of marinade. Cook, stirring constantly until boiling. Pour over the meat in the casserole, cover and cook for 1 hour in a moderate oven (350° F, 180° C). Add the onions and the carrots and continue to cook with the lid on for another hour. Serve with a parsley garnish.

Meat and Potato Casserole

6 medium potatoes cooked and
  sliced
salt and pepper
12 oz or 340 g can luncheon
  meat sliced
⅓ cup sliced green pepper
⅓ cup diced celery
2 tablespoons minced parsley
butter
3 eggs
½ cup milk
½ cup grated Cheddar cheese

Arrange one-third of the potato slices in the bottom of a well-greased casserole and season with salt and pepper. Arrange half the meat slices on the potato and sprinkle with half each of the green pepper, celery and parsley. Add another third of the potato slices, then the remaining meat, green pepper, celery and parsley. Top with the remaining potato slices and dot with butter. Cover and cook in a moderate oven (350° F, 180° C) for about 10 minutes.

Beat the eggs lightly, combine with the milk and season with salt and pepper. Pour the mixture over the ingredients in the casserole and cover and cook in the oven for a further 30 minutes. Remove the lid and sprinkle with the cheese. Return the casserole to the oven to lightly brown and melt the cheese.

Beef Paupiettes ▶
with Mushrooms

*Meat and
Potato Casserole*

Meatball and Potato Casserole

1½ lb or 750 g finely minced
   steak
½ cup soft white breadcrumbs
¼ cup chopped onion
1 teaspoon salt
¼ teaspoon pepper
1 egg
1 teaspoon Worcester sauce
butter for frying
¼ cup chopped onion
15½ oz or 439 g can cream of
   mushroom soup
½ soup can unsweetened canned
   milk
1 cup cooked sliced carrots

Combine the minced steak, breadcrumbs, onion,
salt and pepper and bind with the beaten egg
and the Worcester sauce. Take spoonfuls and
shape into balls about 1½ inches in diameter—it
makes about 18 balls. A little seasoned flour
may be used for shaping.

Heat the butter in a pan and brown the meatballs well. Lift out and place in a lightly greased
casserole. Fry the onions in the butter left in the
pan (add a little more butter if necessary) until
they are golden brown. Now add the soup and
milk and stir until boiling.

Place the carrots and the parsley in the casserole
and pour over the mushroom soup mixture.
Cover and cook in a moderate oven (350° F,

1 tablespoon chopped parsley
4 medium potatoes cooked
melted butter
grated cheese
sesame seeds

180° C) for 20 minutes.

Cut the potatoes into thick slices. Remove the casserole from the oven, top with the potato slices, brush with butter, sprinkle with cheese and sesame seeds and return the dish to the oven uncovered to lightly brown the potatoes.

Meatball Crock

2 tablespoons chopped dried
  onions
$\frac{1}{4}$ cup hot water
1 lb or 500 g finely minced steak
$\frac{1}{4}$ cup day-old breadcrumbs
1 egg
1 teaspoon salt
$\frac{1}{4}$ teaspoon pepper
1 tablespoon Worcester sauce
$\frac{1}{4}$ cup plain flour
2 tablespoons oil
1 large onion peeled and cut into
  chunks
1 medium carrot scraped and
  cut into chunks
2 medium potatoes peeled and
  cut into chunks
$\frac{1}{2}$ lb or 250 g French beans cut
  into 1-inch lengths
$\frac{3}{4}$ cup water
1 teaspoon salt
$1\frac{1}{4}$ cups tomato soup
1 tablespoon beef bouillon or
  yeast extract

Soak the onion in the hot water for 15 minutes. Drain well. Combine the minced steak, breadcrumbs, onion, beaten egg, salt, pepper and Worcester sauce in a bowl. Mix well. Shape into 16 balls using the flour.

Heat the oil in a large pan and fry the meatballs gently until brown. Add the prepared vegetables, water, salt, and tomato soup. Bring to the boil, then transfer to a lightly greased casserole. Cover and cook in a moderate oven (350° F, 180° C) for about 1 hour or until the meat and vegetables are cooked. Just before serving blend the beef bouillon or the yeast extract with a little of the hot gravy and add to the casserole. Reheat before serving.

Mexican Casserole

$1\frac{1}{2}$ lb or 750 g good stewing
  steak
$1\frac{1}{2}$ tablespoons plain flour
$\frac{3}{4}$ teaspoon salt
$\frac{1}{4}$ teaspoon pepper
2 teaspoons brown sugar

Cut the steak into 1-inch cubes and toss in a mixture of flour, salt, pepper, brown sugar and mustard. Prepare the vegetables, cutting only the tops from the shallots. Place alternate layers of meat and vegetables in a lightly greased casserole, then pour over the water or stock and the Wor-

½ teaspoon mustard
2 carrots scraped and cut into chunky pieces
3 medium tomatoes sliced
½ lb or 250 g peas
6 shallots
1½ cups water or stock
1 tablespoon Worcester sauce

cester sauce. Cover and cook in a moderate oven (350° F, 180° C) for about 2 hours.

Mexican Casserole

Minced Steak Casserole

4 medium potatoes
1 medium onion
salt and pepper
2 tablespoons chopped parsley
1 tablespoon plain flour
1 lb or 500 g finely minced steak
½ cup tomato soup
½ cup water

Wash and peel the potatoes and cut into thin slices. Peel and slice the onion. In a large, lightly greased casserole arrange a layer of potato slices, top with onion slices, and season with salt and pepper to taste. Add the parsley and flour. Over this place a layer of minced steak. Top with the remaining potato slices.

Combine the tomato soup and the water and pour over the layers in the casserole. Cover and cook in a moderate oven (350° F, 180° C) for about 45 minutes. Remove the lid and cook for a further 15 minutes to lightly brown the top layer of potatoes.

Pepperpot Steak

1½ lb or 750 g good stewing
  steak
1 or 2 sheep's kidneys
2 rashers of bacon
2 tablespoons plain flour
1 teaspoon salt
good pinch of pepper
1 teaspoon paprika
2 tablespoons butter
1 onion peeled and finely chopped

Cut the steak into cubes. Soak the kidneys in warm water for about 30 minutes, then drain. Dry the kidneys, remove and discard the skin and the white tubes, and chop into ¼-inch pieces. Remove the rind and cut the bacon into 1-inch pieces. Combine the flour, salt, pepper and paprika and toss the bacon, steak and kidney in the mixture.

Heat the butter in a large pan and fry the onion until lightly browned. Add the green pepper and

Pepperpot Steak

1 green pepper seeded and finely
  chopped
1 cup warm water
2 teaspoons instant stock powder
2 tablespoons red wine
1 good sized tomato peeled and
  sliced
1 carrot diced
1 teaspoon brown sugar

sauté for a few minutes, then remove both and place in a casserole. In the same pan, adding a little more butter if necessary, brown the steak then transfer it to the casserole.

Pour the warm water, instant stock and wine into the pan. Bring to the boil, stirring constantly and scraping any browned pieces from the bottom of the pan. Pour over the meat in the casserole and add the tomato, carrot and brown sugar. Cover and cook in a moderate oven (350° F, 180° C) for about 2 hours.

Pinwheel Steaks

$1\frac{1}{2}$ lb or 750 g round steak
$\frac{1}{2}$ lb or 250 g sausage mince
$\frac{1}{2}$ teaspoon salt
pinch of pepper
2 tablespoons chopped shallot
2 tablespoons chopped parsley
2 tablespoons butter
1 tablespoon plain flour
$\frac{3}{4}$ cup stock, or water and 1
  soup cube
1 tablespoon tomato sauce
extra salt and pepper
2 cups diced mixed vegetables
  (carrot, parsnip, celery and
  onion)
2 or 3 bacon rashers (optional)

Trim the meat and cut it into serving pieces, then flatten with a rolling pin or meat mallet. Season the sausage mince with the $\frac{1}{2}$ teaspoon salt and a pinch of pepper, add the chopped shallot and parsley and mix well. Spread some of this filling over each piece of steak and roll up, securing with a wooden cocktail pick.

Heat the butter in a pan and brown the stuffed rolls on all sides. Lift out and keep hot. Add the flour to the fat left in the pan, stir until smooth then cook until brown. Add the stock and tomato sauce and stir until boiling. Taste and add salt and pepper.

Arrange the diced vegetables on the bottom of a lightly greased casserole and top with the browned meat rolls. Pour over the gravy and add the bacon which has had the rind removed and the rashers cut into 1-inch pieces. Cover and cook in a moderate oven (350° F, 180° C) for $1\frac{1}{2}$ hours or until the meat is tender (the bacon is optional but if it has been used, remove the lid for the last 15 minutes of cooking). Remove the cocktail picks from the rolls before serving.

Porcupine Meatballs

1 packet beef-flavoured savoury
  rice
$\frac{3}{4}$ lb or 750 g finely minced steak

Mix the savoury rice with the minced steak, sausage mince and vinegar in a large bowl. Take spoonfuls and shape into balls with dampened

¼ lb or 125 g sausage-mince
1 tablespoon malt vinegar
10½ oz or 298 g can condensed
   tomato soup
1 soup can water
2 tablespoons dry sherry
1 tablespoon Worcester sauce

hands. Place the meatballs in a lightly greased casserole. Heat together the tomato soup, water, sherry and Worcester sauce and pour over the meatballs in the casserole. Cover and cook in a moderate oven (350° F, 180° C) for 1 hour.

Pot Roast Romaine

1 rolled rib of beef
1 or 2 cloves of garlic
¼ cup olive oil or melted butter
3 cloves
1 bouquet garni
4 medium tomatoes
2 cups chopped celery
1 cup red wine
salt and pepper
2 tablespoons plain flour

Make small slits in the surface of the beef and insert small pieces of garlic. Heat the oil or butter in a heavy iron casserole, add the roast and cook, turning frequently until it has coloured on all sides. Add the cloves, bouquet garni, peeled and chopped tomatoes, celery pieces and red wine. Cover and cook in a moderate oven (350° F, 180° C) for about 2 hours or until the meat is tender (beef is usually preferred rare, so be careful not to overcook). Lift the meat out.

Strain the liquid from the casserole into a saucepan and add the salt and pepper. Blend the flour with a little stock, water or wine and add to the liquid. Stir over moderate heat until boiling.

If the casserole is large enough, carrots and potatoes may be cooked with the meat.

Rice and Meatball Casserole

1 lb or 500 g finely minced beef
½ cup uncooked rice
1 tablespoon finely chopped onion
½ teaspoon dried basil
⅓ cup grated cheese
1½ teaspoons salt
¼ teaspoon pepper
½ cup milk
2 tablespoons oil
15½ oz or 439 g can cream of
   tomato soup

Combine the minced beef, rice, onion, basil, grated cheese, salt, pepper and milk. Blend well, then chill for about 30 minutes. Take spoonfuls and shape into balls (you should have about 20). Brown a few at a time in the heated oil. As they are browned drain them on paper and place in a casserole. Now add the soup, water, sauce and green pepper. Bake uncovered in a moderate to hot oven (400° F, 200° C) for 35 minutes. Add the cooked peas and carrots, then cover and cook for a further 35 minutes.

1 soup can water
¼ teaspoon Worcester sauce
½ cup chopped green pepper
½ cup cooked green peas
2 cups sliced cooked carrots

Rice and Meatball Casserole

Rich Beef Casserole

2 lb or 1 kg round or good
   stewing steak
4 slices bacon
2 or 3 onions peeled and sliced
salt and pepper
1 clove of garlic crushed
pinch of marjoram
½ cup red wine
1¼ cups water or stock
3 carrots scraped and sliced
2 parsnips scraped and sliced
1 tablespoon flour creamed with
   1 teaspoon butter

Cut the steak into cubes. Remove the rind and
cut the bacon into pieces, then fry in a pan until
the fat is clear. Lift out and place in a casserole.
Add the onions to the bacon fat left in the pan
and cook until brown. Lift out and place in the
casserole.

Put the steak into the casserole and add salt
and pepper to taste, and the garlic, marjoram,
wine and stock. Cover and cook in a moderate
oven (350° F, 180° C) for about 1½ hours. Add
the vegetables and replace in the oven to cook for
another 30 minutes. Stir in the blended flour and
butter, cover and return the casserole to the oven
to cook for a further 15 minutes.

Romany Beef Balls

1 lb or 500 g finely minced beef
1 cup soft white breadcrumbs
1 rounded tablespoon minced
 onion
2 teaspoons fruit chutney
2 teaspoons chopped parsley
good pinch of herbs
½ teaspoon salt
dash of pepper
1 egg
2 tablespoons plain flour
½ teaspoon salt
½ teaspoon dry mustard
1 teaspoon brown sugar
1 cup water or stock
½ teaspoon Parisian essence
bacon rashers (optional)

Combine the minced beef, breadcrumbs, onion, chutney, parsley, herbs, salt and pepper and bind with a little beaten egg. Take spoonfuls of the mixture and form into 8 balls in the palms of the hands. Mix the flour with the salt, mustard and brown sugar and use to thoroughly coat the meatballs.

Arrange the balls in a lightly greased casserole. Combine the water or stock with the Parisian essence and any left-over flour mixture, pour over the meat and top, if liked, with bacon rashers. Bake uncovered in a moderate oven (350° F, 180° C) for about 45 minutes. Serve with fluffy mashed potatoes and green peas.

Savoury Steak Casserole

1 rasher of bacon
2 lb or 1 kg good stewing steak
2 tablespoons seasoned plain flour
1 cup diced carrots
1 cup diced parsnips
1 cup diced onion
½ cup diced celery
1 clove of garlic crushed
1 cup beef stock, or water and
 1 soup cube
2 teaspoons Worcester sauce
2 teaspoons soy sauce
2 teaspoons brown sugar
¼ teaspoon salt
dash of pepper

Remove the rind and cut the bacon into 1-inch pieces. Place in a heavy-based pan and cook until the fat is clear. Remove the bacon from the pan, draining well.

Remove any excess fat and cut the meat into 1-inch cubes. Coat well with seasoned flour. Add the steak to the bacon fat in the pan and cook, stirring well, until the meat has browned. Remove to a lightly greased casserole and add the bacon.

To any fat left in the pan add the vegetables and the garlic. Cook, stirring lightly, until the vegetables have a glazed appearance (you may need to add a little more fat). Stir in any remaining flour and cook until it has browned, then add the beef stock, sauces, brown sugar, salt and pepper. When the mixture comes to the boil pour it over the meat and bacon in the casserole. Cover and cook in a moderate oven (350° F, 180° C) for about 2 hours or until the meat is tender.

Simplicity Casserole

4 teaspoons instant onion stock
   powder
1½ tablespoons plain flour
pinch of pepper
1 lb or 500 g stewing steak
1 cup cold water
1 large carrot
2 stalks celery
salt

Mix the instant stock with the plain flour and pepper. Cut the meat into cubes and toss them in the seasoned flour. Place in a casserole, add the water and stir until well mixed, then add the carrots which have been scraped and cut into slices, and the celery which has been washed and cut into ½-inch pieces. Cover and cook in a moderate oven (350° F, 180° C) for about 2 hours or until the meat is tender.

Taste and add salt if necessary (the instant stock powder contains a fair amount of salt).

Steak a la Mode

2 lb or 1 kg good stewing steak
2 tablespoons seasoned plain
   flour
margarine or fat for frying
1 onion sliced
2 carrots sliced
1½ cups stock, or water and 1
   soup cube or instant stock
   powder
1 teaspoon salt
dash of pepper
½ level teaspoon dry mustard
1 teaspoon brown sugar
1 tablespoon Worcester sauce
1 tablespoon tomato sauce
parsley to garnish

Trim the meat, cut into cubes, and toss them in the seasoned flour. Heat the margarine in a heavy-based pan and fry the meat until brown on all sides. Lift out with a slotted spoon and place in a casserole.

Put the sliced onion and carrots in the pan and sauté for about 5 minutes, then stir in any flour left over from the meat. Cook until brown. Add the water and stir until the liquid boils and thickens slightly. Crumble in the soup cube and add the salt, pepper, mustard, brown sugar and sauces. Stir again until boiling, then pour over the meat in the casserole. Cover and cook in a moderate oven (350° F, 180° C) for about 2 hours or until the meat is tender. Serve with a parsley garnish.

Steak and Potato Casserole

2 lb or 1 kg round steak about
   1 inch thick
2 teaspoons salt
dash of pepper
plain flour

Trim the meat of any excess fat and cut it into cubes. Season with salt and pepper and coat with flour. Sauté the onions in the melted butter, remove and set aside.

Brown the meat in the same pan, then transfer

4 medium onions thinly sliced
¼ cup butter
15 oz or 425 g can undiluted
    tomato soup
1 bay-leaf
3 large potatoes peeled and
    halved or quartered

to a casserole. Pour the soup into the pan and stir until boiling, scraping any brown pieces from the pan. Add the onions and the bay-leaf. Pour over the meat and add the potatoes. Cover and cook in a moderate oven (350° F, 180° C) for about 1½ hours or until the meat is tender.

Steak and Tomato Casserole 1

3 rashers of bacon
2 lb or 1 kg good stewing steak
2 tablespoons seasoned plain flour
1 clove of garlic crushed
2 or 3 good-sized tomatoes
    peeled and sliced
1 cup chopped onion
1 cup chopped celery
2 tablespoons claret or burgundy
1 teaspoon Worcester sauce
2 teaspoons brown sugar
½ cup water
1 soup cube
1 tablespoon soy sauce
1 teaspoon salt
¼ teaspoon pepper

Remove the rind and cut the bacon into 1-inch pieces. Fry until the fat is clear and the bacon crisp. Remove and drain on paper.

Cut the steak into 1-inch cubes and coat with seasoned flour. Fry lightly in the bacon fat left in the pan. Lift out and place in a casserole with the bacon, garlic, tomato slices, onion and celery. Combine the wine with the Worcester sauce, brown sugar, soup cube, water, soy sauce, salt and pepper, and pour over the contents of the casserole. Cover and cook in a moderate oven (350° F, 180° C) for 1½ to 2 hours or until the meat is tender.

Steak and Tomato Casserole 2

2 lb or 1 kg round or buttock
    steak
2 tablespoons plain flour
1 teaspoon salt
pinch of pepper
2 tablespoons butter or fat
1 medium onion peeled and
    sliced
1 clove of garlic peeled and
    crushed
4 medium tomatoes sliced

Remove any excess fat or gristle from the meat and cut into cubes. Toss it in the flour, salt and pepper. Heat the butter in a pan and fry the onion until golden. Lift out, add the meat and cook quickly to brown on all sides, then sprinkle with the remainder of the flour. Cook for a few minutes, then add the garlic, tomato slices, 1 teaspoon of the tomato paste, the stock and the oregano. Stir until boiling. Turn the mixture into a casserole and add the onion. Cover and cook in a moderate oven (350° F, 180° C) for about 1¾

2 teaspoons tomato paste
¾ cup stock, or water and 1 soup
  cube
pinch of oregano
2 tablespoons white wine

hours. Blend the remaining teaspoon of tomato paste with the white wine and stir into the casserole. Replace the lid and continue to cook until the meat is tender.

Steak and Walnuts

1½ lb or 750 g good stewing steak
2 tablespoons seasoned plain flour
1 tablespoon fat
1¼ cups water or stock
6 pickled walnuts
finely chopped parsley to garnish

Cut the steak into cubes and toss in the seasoned flour. Fry in the hot fat in a heavy-based pan until brown, then lift out and place in a casserole.

Add any remaining flour to the pan and stir over moderate heat until brown. Add the water or stock and stir until the mixture boils and thickens slightly. Pour over the meat in the casserole. Cover and cook in a moderate oven (350° F, 180° C) for about 1 hour. Cut the pickled walnuts into quarters and place in the casserole together with 1 tablespoon of the liquid from the jar of walnuts. Continue to cook with the lid on until the steak is tender. Serve sprinkled with chopped parsley.

Stifado

2 lb or 1 kg buttock steak
2 teaspoons salt
freshly ground black pepper
2 oz or 60 g butter
12 small white onions
⅓ cup claret
1 tablespoon red wine vinegar
½ cup tomato paste
1 tablespoon light brown sugar
1 tablespoon beef bouillon
1 small clove of garlic peeled
  and crushed
1 small bay-leaf
1 small stick cinnamon
4 cloves
1 tablespoon raisins

Cut the meat into 1-inch pieces and season it with the salt and some freshly ground black pepper. Melt the butter in a pan and add the steak. Cook just long enough to coat the meat with butter—do not brown. Transfer the meat to a casserole.

Measure any liquid left in the pan and make it up to ½ cup with water. Pour this over the meat. Peel the onions and place on top of the meat. Mix together the claret, red wine vinegar, tomato paste, brown sugar, beef bouillon, and crushed garlic and pour this over the meat and onions. Add the bay-leaf, cinnamon stick and cloves. Sprinkle the raisins on top. Cover and cook in a moderately slow oven (325° F, 160° C) for 2 to 2½ hours or until the meat and onions are tender.

Swedish Beef Rolls

2 lb or 1 kg round steak
salt and pepper
prepared mustard
seasoned plain flour
$\frac{1}{4}$ cup butter
3 tablespoons chopped onions
2 cups beef stock, or water and
   2 soup cubes
$\frac{1}{4}$ cup milk
$\frac{1}{4}$ cup cream
$1\frac{1}{2}$ slightly rounded tablespoons
   plain flour

Trim off the excess fat and cut the meat into 2-inch squares. Pound with a meat mallet until each piece is about 4 inches square. Sprinkle with salt and pepper and spread each square lightly with prepared mustard. Fold in the edges of the steak and roll up tightly to make the rolls about 2 inches long. Secure with wooden cocktail picks.

Coat each roll with seasoned flour and brown in the heated butter in a heavy-based frying pan, then lift out. Add the onion to the pan and cook until lightly browned, then pour in the stock and stir until boiling. Place the browned rolls in a lightly greased casserole, pour over the gravy, cover and cook in a moderate oven (350° F, 180° C) for about $1\frac{1}{2}$ hours.

Combine the cream and milk (or use all milk) and blend with the plain flour. Remove the casserole from the oven and stir in the milk and cream mixture, making sure it is mixed in evenly. Replace the cover and return the casserole to the oven to cook for a further 15 minutes. Remove the cocktail picks before serving.

Sweet and Sour Beef

2 lb or 1 kg round steak cut into
   1-inch cubes
seasoned plain flour
1 tablespoon butter or oil
1 teaspoon salt
$\frac{1}{2}$ cup chopped onion
$\frac{3}{4}$ cup water
1 clove of garlic peeled and
   crushed
$\frac{1}{2}$ cup tomato purée
$\frac{1}{3}$ cup vinegar
$\frac{1}{3}$ cup brown sugar
2 teaspoons mixed mustard
2 cups cubed mixed vegetables
   (carrot, parsnip, potato and
   green pepper)

Toss the meat cubes in the seasoned flour, then brown them in the hot butter or oil in a heavy-based pan or in a top-of-the-stove casserole. Season with the salt and add the onion. Cook, stirring constantly, until lightly browned. Add the water and stir until boiling. Transfer to a casserole if the meat has been browned in a pan, cover and cook in a moderate oven (350° F, 180° C) for 1 hour.

Add the garlic, tomato purée, vinegar, brown sugar and mustard, then the mixed vegetables. Cover, return to the oven and cook for a further hour. Serve with orange rice.

Orange Rice

Place 1 cup rice, $1\frac{1}{2}$ cups cold water, $\frac{1}{2}$ cup orange juice, 1 teaspoon salt and 2 teaspoons grated

Sweet and Sour Beef

orange rind in a large saucepan with a tightly fitting lid. Bring to the boil, stirring once or twice during this period, then lower the heat and simmer very gently for another 15 minutes without removing the lid. The water will have been absorbed by the rice, which should not need draining.

Swiss Bliss

2 lb or 1 kg buttock steak
1 packet onion soup mix
$\frac{1}{2}$ lb or 250 g mushrooms sliced
$\frac{1}{2}$ green pepper seeded and sliced
15 oz or 425 g can tomatoes peeled and chopped (reserve the liquid)
$\frac{1}{4}$ teaspoon salt
good pinch of pepper
$\frac{1}{2}$ cup juice from canned tomatoes
2 teaspoons Worcester sauce
2 teaspoons cornflour
1 tablespoon chopped parsley to garnish

Cut the steak into cubes and place in a lightly greased casserole. Sprinkle over the onion soup mix, the mushrooms, green pepper and tomatoes. Season with salt and pepper. Blend together the tomato liquid, Worcester sauce and cornflour and add to the casserole. Cover and cook in a moderate oven (350° F, 180° C) for 2 hours or until the meat is tender. Sprinkle with the chopped parsley before serving.

37

Swiss Pepper Steak

1½ lb or 750 g blade or round
    steak cut in 2 pieces
2 tablespoons plain flour
2 teaspoons salad oil
2 small green peppers seeded and
    cut into strips
1 onion peeled and sliced
4 medium tomatoes peeled and
    sliced
salt and pepper
2 stalks celery chopped
1 beef soup cube
1 bay-leaf crumbled
½ cup stock or water

Coat the two pieces of meat with the flour. Heat the oil in a heavy-based pan and brown the meat on both sides. Remove from the pan and place one piece in the bottom of a lightly greased casserole. Arrange on it half the green pepper strips, half the onion slices and half the tomato slices. Season with salt and pepper and add any left-over flour.

Place the remaining piece of steak on top and add the rest of the pepper strips, onion slices and tomato slices. Cover with the diced celery, the crumbled soup cube and bay-leaf, then pour over the stock. Put the lid on and cook in a moderate oven (350° F, 180° C) for 1½ to 2 hours or until the steak is tender.

Almond Chicken Curry

2 medium roasting chickens
1 onion
6 peppercorns
1 teaspoon salt
1 bay-leaf
½ cup butter
2 medium cloves of garlic
   crushed in 1 teaspoon salt
2 cups sliced onion rings
2 tablespoons curry powder
2 tablespoons (slightly rounded)
   plain flour
2 cups chicken stock (liquid in
   which chickens were cooked)
½ cup unsweetened canned milk
1 egg
2 tablespoons chutney
½ cup halved toasted almonds

Cut the chicken into serving pieces and place in a saucepan with the onion, peppercorns, salt and bay-leaf and enough cold water to partly cover. Place the lid on the saucepan and simmer until the flesh is just tender. Lift out the chicken pieces and cool the liquid in which they were cooked. If liked, the flesh may be removed from the bones.

Melt the butter in a medium-sized saucepan and fry the chicken until brown. Lift out and place in a lightly greased casserole. Sauté the garlic and the onion rings in the same pan, then remove with a slotted spoon and place with the chicken. Stir the curry powder and flour into the butter in the pan, cook for 2 minutes then add the chicken stock and stir until the mixture boils and thickens. Pour over the chicken. Cover and cook in a moderate oven (350° F, 180° C) for about 15 minutes. Beat the unsweetened canned milk with the egg and stir into the casserole. Add chutney to taste and sprinkle with the almonds. Serve with freshly boiled rice.

Barbecued Chicken Casserole

1 large roasting chicken
½ cup plain flour
2 teaspoons salt
¼ cup salad oil or butter
1 medium onion sliced
½ cup chopped celery
¼ cup minced green pepper
½ cup tomato sauce
1 cup stock, or water and 1 soup cube
½ tablespoon Worcester sauce
½ tablespoon brown sugar
good pinch of pepper
1 packet frozen corn kernels

Cut the chicken into neat serving pieces and toss each piece in a mixture of flour and salt. Brown in the hot oil or butter in a heavy-based pan. Drain and place in a casserole.

With only ½ tablespoon of oil in the pan add the onion and cook until golden. Stir in the celery, green pepper, tomato sauce, stock, Worcester sauce, brown sugar and pepper. When boiling, pour over the chicken and if time permits, let stand for several hours. Cover and cook in a moderate oven (350° F, 180° C) for about 1½ hours. Add the corn, cover again and cook in the oven for 20 minutes longer or until the chicken is tender.

Brown Chicken Casserole

1 large roasting chicken
seasoned plain flour
butter for frying
1 onion peeled and sliced
1 tablespoon butter (for gravy)
1 rounded tablespoon plain flour
1½ cups chicken stock
2 teaspoons tomato paste
salt and pepper
1 teaspoon Worcester sauce
½ cup sliced celery
1 cup sliced carrots
¾ cup sliced mushrooms
1 cup cooked green peas
chopped parsley to garnish

Cut the chicken into neat serving pieces and coat them with seasoned flour. Sauté in a little butter in a heavy-based pan until lightly browned. Drain well and place in a greased casserole.

Fry the sliced onion in the butter remaining in the pan until golden in colour, then add to the chicken in the casserole. Melt the tablespoon of butter in the same pan, then stir in the flour. Cook, stirring constantly, until it browns lightly, then add the stock and tomato paste and stir until boiling. Now add the salt, pepper, Worcester sauce, celery, carrots and mushrooms. Bring to the boil and pour over the chicken in the casserole. Cover and cook at 350° F (180° C) for about 1½ hours or until the chicken is tender. About 15 minutes before serving, add the cooked green peas. Serve with a chopped parsley garnish.

Chicken a l'Orange

8 chicken pieces
$\frac{1}{3}$ cup plain flour
1 teaspoon salt
$\frac{1}{4}$ teaspoon pepper
2 oz or 60 g butter
1 small onion peeled and minced
$\frac{3}{4}$ cup water
1 soup cube or 1 teaspoon
   instant chicken stock
$\frac{1}{2}$ cup orange juice
1 teaspoon grated orange rind
parsley and thin slices of orange
   to garnish

Dust the chicken pieces with a mixture of flour, salt and pepper. Heat the butter in a heavy-based pan and fry the chicken pieces until brown on both sides. Lift out, drain on paper and place in a lightly greased casserole.

Sauté the minced onion in the butter left in the pan (add a little more butter if necessary) for about 5 minutes. Sprinkle in any remaining flour and stir over medium heat until brown, then gradually add the water, soup cube or instant stock and the orange juice. Stir until boiling, then add the grated rind. Pour this gravy over the browned chicken pieces in the casserole. Cover and cook in a moderate oven (350° F, 180° C) for about 1 hour or until the chicken is tender. Serve garnished with un-peeled orange slices and parsley sprigs and accompany with freshly boiled rice.

Chicken a la King

15 oz or 425 g can cream of
   celery soup
1 cup grated cheese
1 tablespoon butter
2 tablespoons finely chopped
   green pepper
2 cups diced cooked chicken
2 tablespoons finely chopped
   shallots
$\frac{1}{4}$ teaspoon dry mustard
dash of pepper
1 teaspoon curry powder
2 teaspoons lemon juice
4 oz or 125 g noodles cooked
   and drained
asparagus spears for topping

Place the undiluted soup in a saucepan and bring to the boil. Add the grated cheese and stir until it has melted. Melt the butter in a saucepan, add the green pepper and shallots, and sauté

Chicken a la King

◀ *Meatball and Potato Casserole*

until both are soft. Add to the soup mixture, then stir in the chicken, mustard, pepper, curry powder and lemon juice.

Turn the mixture into a lightly greased casserole and arrange the cooked noodles on top. Cover with the well-drained asparagus spears, put the lid on and cook in a moderate oven (350° F, 180° C) for about 20 minutes or until thoroughly heated.

Chicken and Egg Casserole

¼ cup chopped green pepper
2 teaspoons butter
10½ oz or 298 g can cream of
  celery soup
½ cup milk
1 cup diced cooked chicken
4 hard-boiled eggs peeled and
  quartered
1 tablespoon chopped canned
  pimento
¼ cup fine breadcrumbs
1 tablespoon melted butter

Sauté the green pepper in the butter until tender, then stir in the soup and milk. Heat, stirring until boiling. Add to it the chicken, eggs and pimento. Turn the mixture into a lightly greased casserole.

Toss the breadcrumbs and the melted butter in a saucepan over medium heat until the crumbs have absorbed the butter, then sprinkle them on top of the casserole. Bake uncovered in a moderate oven (350° F, 180° C) until the sauce bubbles and the crumbs brown—about 20 or 30 minutes.

Chicken and Ham Casserole

1½ tablespoons butter
1 tablespoon chopped shallot
2 slightly rounded tablespoons
  plain flour
¼ teaspoon white pepper
1 teaspoon salt
¼ teaspoon paprika
1½ cups milk, or half milk and
  half chicken stock
½ cup cream
2½ cups coarsely chopped cooked
  chicken
1 cup chopped ham
buttered breadcrumbs
grated cheese
parsley to garnish

Melt the butter in a saucepan and add the shallot. Sauté until soft but not brown. Add the flour, pepper, salt and paprika and stir until smooth, then cook for 1 minute without browning. Add the milk or milk mixture and cook, stirring constantly, until the sauce boils and thickens, then add the cream. Simmer for 2 minutes.

Stir in the chicken and ham and place in a lightly greased casserole. Top with the buttered breadcrumbs and a little grated cheese. Bake uncovered in a moderate oven (350° F, 180° C) until the cheese melts, the crumbs brown and the sauce bubbles. Serve with a parsley garnish.

Chicken and Potato Casserole

4 cups thinly sliced potatoes
1 slightly rounded tablespoon
    plain flour
1 teaspoon salt
good pinch of seasoned pepper
1 large onion peeled and thinly
    sliced
1 tablespoon butter
1½ cups milk
2 rashers of bacon
1 large roasting chicken
paprika

Grease a casserole and place a layer of sliced potatoes on the bottom. Combine the flour, salt and pepper and sprinkle half over the potatoes. Add half the onion slices, dot with butter then add another layer of potatoes, seasoned flour and onions. Pour the milk over the whole. Cover and place in a moderate oven while preparing the chicken.

Cut the chicken into neat serving pieces and sauté them in melted butter in a heavy-based pan until brown. Lift out and place on top of the potatoes in the casserole. Fry the bacon in the same pan and use to top the chicken. Cover and cook in a moderate oven (350° F, 180° C) for about 1 hour or until the chicken is tender. Uncover, add a little more milk if necessary and sprinkle with paprika before serving.

Chicken Bearnais

1 large roasting chicken
seasoned plain flour
2 tablespoons butter
1 tablespoon oil
2 medium onions peeled and
    chopped
1 lb 12 oz or 794 g can peeled
    tomatoes
1 tablespoon tomato paste
4 rashers of bacon with rind
    removed
1 cup sliced mushrooms
4 tablespoons dry white wine

Cut the chicken into serving pieces and toss each piece in seasoned flour. Heat the butter and oil in a heavy-based pan and fry the chicken pieces until a golden brown all over. Lift out, drain on paper and place in a lightly greased casserole. Add the onions to the butter and oil left in the pan and cook, stirring constantly, until golden. Lift out with a slotted spoon and sprinkle over the chicken in the casserole.

Combine the tomatoes and tomato paste and add to the casserole. Using the same pan, fry the bacon (which has been cut into 1-inch pieces) until the fat is clear, then add the mushrooms and sauté lightly. Pour on the wine and when boiling add to the casserole. Cover and cook in a moderate oven (350° F, 180° C) for 1 hour or until the chicken is tender.

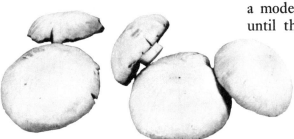

43

Chicken Bonne Femme

2 lb or 1 kg chicken breasts
2 tablespoons plain flour
½ teaspoon salt
3 rashers of bacon
1 tablespoon butter
4 oz or 125 g button mushrooms
12 spring onions chopped
1 cup chicken stock
½ cup white wine
1 bouquet garni (1 sprig thyme,
    1 bay-leaf, 1 stalk celery,
    2 sprigs parsley)
2 or 3 medium potatoes or 8
    baby new potatoes
chopped parsley to garnish

Remove the bones from the chicken breasts and roll the pieces in the flour and salt. Remove the rind and cut the bacon into bite-sized pieces and fry in a heavy-based pan until the flesh is crisp and the fat clear. Lift out with a slotted spoon.

Add the chicken to the pan and brown lightly on all sides. Lift out, add the butter, mushrooms and chopped spring onion. Cook, stirring constantly, until the onion begins to colour. Lift out and place in the casserole with the bacon and chicken.

Add any flour left from coating the chicken and cook for a few minutes. Add the stock and wine. Cook, stirring constantly, until the liquid boils and thickens. Pour over the contents of the casserole, add the bouquet garni, cover and cook in a moderate oven (350° F, 180° C) for 30 minutes. Add the potatoes (if using the larger ones cut them in four first). Cover again and cook for a further 30 minutes or until both the chicken and vegetables are tender. Remove the bouquet garni and serve accompanied with freshly boiled rice and plenty of chopped parsley.

Chicken Cacciatore

1 large roasting chicken
2 tablespoons seasoned plain
    flour
2 tablespoons cooking oil
½ cup minced onion
1 clove of garlic crushed
3 tomatoes quartered
1 tablespoon tomato paste
¼ cup chicken stock
¼ cup dry white wine
salt and pepper
1 large bay-leaf tied with 3 sprigs
    of parsley and 1 of thyme
¼ lb or 125 g mushrooms sliced

Cut the chicken into neat serving pieces. Use the carcass to make the chicken stock. Coat the chicken pieces with seasoned flour and fry in the oil in a heavy-based pan until lightly browned. Lift out and place in a casserole.

Fry the onion in the oil left in the pan, then add to the casserole with the garlic, tomatoes, tomato paste, stock, wine, salt and pepper to taste and the bouquet of herbs. Cover and cook in a moderate oven (350° F, 180° C) for about 45 minutes. Add the sliced mushrooms to the casserole and cover and cook for a further 15 minutes or until tender. Serve with buttered spaghetti or with spaghetti seasoned with tomato paste.

44

Chicken Carnival

4 large chicken thighs
2 large tomatoes diced
1 cup cauliflower flowerets
10 oz or 283 g can asparagus tips
  drained
2 tablespoons tomato paste
freshly ground black pepper
garlic salt
$\frac{3}{4}$ cup coarsely grated cheese

Arrange all the ingredients except the cheese in a lightly greased casserole. Cover and cook in a fairly hot oven (400° F, 200° C) for 1 hour. Remove the lid and bake uncovered for a further 30 minutes or until the chicken is tender. Sprinkle with the cheese, then replace in the oven or put under the griller to melt and lightly brown the cheese.

Chicken Casserole 1

1 large roasting chicken
2 tablespoons seasoned plain
  flour
2 tablespoons oil
1 medium onion peeled and
  sliced
1 clove of garlic crushed
6 small tomatoes peeled and sliced
$\frac{1}{4}$ lb or 125 g mushrooms sliced
2 teaspoons tomato paste
$\frac{1}{2}$ cup chicken stock
salt and pepper
$\frac{1}{2}$ cup white wine or Marsala

Cut the chicken into serving pieces and coat each piece with seasoned flour. Heat the oil in a heavy-based pan and fry the sliced onion until it begins to brown, then add the garlic. Lift out and place in a casserole.

Fry the chicken pieces in the oil left in the pan (add a little more oil if necessary) until they begin to brown, then transfer them to the casserole.

Place the tomato slices and mushroom slices in layers on top of the chicken. Blend the tomato paste, stock, salt, pepper and wine and pour over the contents of the casserole. Cover and cook in a moderate oven (350° F, 180° C) for about 1½ hours or until the chicken is tender.

If liked the gravy may be thickened with a little flour blended with a little butter.

Chicken Casserole 2

2 lb or 1 kg chicken pieces
1 teaspoon salt
$\frac{1}{4}$ teaspoon pepper
$\frac{1}{2}$ cup plain flour
1 tablespoon oil
1 tablespoon butter
1 clove of garlic crushed
$\frac{1}{2}$ cup stock

Coat each piece of chicken with seasoned flour. Heat the oil and butter in a heavy-based pan and brown the chicken pieces on all sides. Lift out and place in a casserole.

Add the garlic, stock and wine to the pan and stir till boiling, scraping up any browned bits which have stuck to the pan. Pour it over the chicken in the casserole. Add the bouquet garni

½ cup white wine
1 bouquet garni
2 large tomatoes skinned and
sliced
1 dozen medium mushrooms
chopped parsley to garnish

then the tomato slices. Cover and cook in a moderate oven (350° F, 180° C) for 45 minutes, then add the mushrooms, cover again and continue cooking until the chicken is tender. Sprinkle with chopped parsley before serving.

Chicken Casserole 3

1 large roasting chicken
2 tablespoons seasoned plain flour
1 tablespoon butter
1 tablespoon oil
1 medium onion peeled and sliced
1 clove of garlic crushed
6 small tomatoes peeled and
sliced
¼ lb or 125 g fresh mushrooms
sliced
1 tablespoon tomato paste
½ cup chicken stock
½ cup white wine
salt and pepper

Cut the chicken into serving pieces. Use the carcass to make the stock. Coat each piece of chicken with seasoned flour and fry until lightly browned in the heated butter and oil in a heavy-based pan. Lift out and place in a casserole.

Fry the onion until golden in the same pan, adding a little more butter if necessary. Lift out and place in the casserole. Add the garlic. Place the tomato and mushroom slices in layers on top of the chicken. Blend the tomato paste with the stock and the wine and season lightly with salt and pepper. Pour over the contents of the casserole. Cover and cook in a moderate oven (350° F, 180° C) for about 1½ hours or until the chicken is tender.

Chicken Casserole 4

1 roasting chicken (about 3 lb
or 1.5 kg)
seasoned plain flour
2 tablespoons butter
2 medium onions peeled and
thinly sliced
1 tablespoon plain flour
salt and cayenne pepper
1 cup chicken stock made from
the carcass
¼ cup white wine
¼ cup tomato purée
parsley to garnish

Cut the chicken into serving pieces and remove as much skin as possible. Coat each portion with seasoned flour. Heat the butter in a heavy-based pan and fry the chicken pieces until brown. Lift out and place in a lightly greased casserole.

Add the onions to the butter remaining in the pan (use a little more butter if necessary) and cook until lightly browned. Stir in the flour and season with salt and cayenne pepper to taste. Cook until the flour browns, then add the chicken stock, white wine and tomato purée. Cook, stirring constantly, until boiling. Pour over the chicken in the casserole, then cover and cook in a moderate oven (350° F, 180° C) for about 1½ hours or until the chicken is tender. Sprinkle with chopped parsley before serving.

46

Chicken Celeste

1 medium-size roasting chicken
$\frac{1}{3}$ cup plain flour
$1\frac{1}{2}$ teaspoons salt
good pinch of pepper
$\frac{1}{4}$ teaspoon paprika
2 oz or 60 g butter or margarine
$\frac{1}{2}$ cup chopped onion
$\frac{1}{2}$ cup dry sherry
$\frac{1}{4}$ cup water
$\frac{1}{2}$ cup fresh cream or cultured
  sour cream
1 tablespoon chopped parsley to
  garnish

Cut the chicken into serving pieces. Combine the flour, salt, pepper and paprika and use to coat the chicken pieces. Heat the butter in a heavy-based pan and fry each portion of chicken well. Lift out and place in a casserole.

Add the onion to the butter left in the pan and sauté it until soft but not brown. Add the sherry and water and bring to the boil. Pour over the chicken in the casserole. Cover and cook in a moderate oven (350° F, 180° C) for about 1 hour. Pour in the cream, stir lightly to mix, and replace in the oven to reheat. Taste and add more salt and pepper if necessary. Sprinkle with chopped parsley before serving.

Chicken Creme Casserole

6 chicken pieces
2 tablespoons seasoned plain
  flour
1 tablespoon butter
$\frac{1}{2}$ cup chopped onion or shallot
$\frac{1}{4}$ teaspoon mixed herbs
salt and pepper
2 medium carrots scraped and
  sliced
$15\frac{1}{4}$ oz or 432 g can cream of
  chicken soup
$\frac{1}{2}$ cup unsweetened evaporated
  milk or cream
1 tablespoon chopped parsley to
  garnish
bacon rolls

Coat the chicken pieces with the seasoned flour then brown them on all sides in the melted butter in a heavy-based pan. Lift out, drain on paper and place in a casserole.

Sauté the onion or shallot in any butter left in the pan (add a little butter if necessary). Add to the casserole, then sprinkle with the herbs, add salt and pepper to taste and then the carrots. Pour over the can of soup, cover and cook in a moderate oven (350° F, 180° C) for about $1\frac{1}{2}$ hours or until the chicken is tender. Stir in the evaporated milk or cream and heat without boiling. Serve sprinkled with chopped parsley and grilled or baked bacon rolls.

Chicken Curry

1 large chicken
butter for frying
seasoned plain flour
2 medium onions peeled and
  chopped

Cut the chicken into neat serving pieces. Heat the butter in a heavy-based pan. Coat the chicken pieces with seasoned flour and fry them until lightly browned on all sides. Lift out, drain on paper and place in a lightly greased casserole.

Chicken en Cocotte/Chicken Curry

1 small apple peeled and diced
2 slightly rounded teaspoons
  curry powder
1 tablespoon plain flour
1 tablespoon chutney
½ teaspoon salt
pinch of allspice
1 tomato peeled and chopped
1 tablespoon coconut
1¼ cups stock made from the
  carcass
1 teaspoon lemon juice

Add the onion to the butter left in the pan (add a little more butter if necessary) and fry until golden. Add the apple and fry lightly, then stir in the curry powder and the flour. Cook, stirring constantly, for about 2 minutes or until the flour begins to colour. Add the chutney, salt, allspice, tomato, coconut and stock. Stir until boiling, then pour over the chicken in the casserole. Cover and cook in a moderate oven (350° F, 180° C) for about 1½ hours or until the chicken is tender. Flavour with the lemon juice and serve with freshly boiled rice and curry accompaniments such as nuts, pineapple, coconut and crisply cooked bacon.

48

Chicken en Cocotte

1 large roasting chicken
3 tablespoons plain flour
salt
freshly ground black pepper
4 rashers of bacon diced
6 shallots chopped
2 medium carrots scraped and
   sliced
1 tablespoon oil
1 tablespoon butter
2 tablespoons heated brandy
4 medium tomatoes peeled and
   sliced
1 bouquet garni
$\frac{1}{2}$ cup chicken stock
$\frac{1}{2}$ cup red wine
parsley to garnish

Cut the chicken into neat serving pieces. Combine 2 tablespoons of the flour with the salt and pepper and use to coat the chicken pieces. Set aside.

In a heavy-based pan brown the diced bacon, lift out and set aside. Add the shallots and carrots to the bacon fat in the pan and cook until soft but not brown. Remove from the pan. Add the oil and butter to the pan and brown the chicken pieces a few at a time. Return all the chicken pieces to the pan, pour over the warmed brandy and ignite. When the flames have died down add the remaining tablespoon of flour and stir until brown. Add the bacon, shallots and carrots, then the sliced tomatoes, bouquet garni, stock and wine. Bring to the boil and transfer to a lightly greased casserole. Cover and cook in a moderate oven (350° F, 180° C) for about $1\frac{1}{2}$ hours or until the chicken is tender. Serve with a parsley garnish.

Chicken Goulash

1 large boiling fowl
seasoned plain flour
butter for frying
6 small white onions (or $\frac{1}{2}$ bunch
   shallots)
2 cloves of garlic crushed
2 teaspoons plain flour
$1\frac{1}{2}$ teaspoons chilli powder
1 teaspoon salt
10 oz or 283 g can condensed
   beef consommé
2 medium carrots scraped and
   sliced
2 cups chunky pieces of
   zucchini
2 medium tomatoes peeled and
   sliced

Cut the fowl into serving pieces and toss them in the seasoned flour. Melt the butter in a heavy-based pan and fry the chicken portions until brown. Lift out, drain on paper and place in a lightly greased casserole.

In the same pan brown the onions and add the garlic. Lift out and add to the casserole.

Sprinkle the plain flour into the pan, add the chilli powder and salt and stir until it browns, then add the consommé and stir until boiling. Pour over the chicken in the casserole and add the carrots. Cover and cook in a moderate oven (350° F, 180° C) for about $1\frac{1}{2}$ hours or until the chicken is tender. Sauté the zucchini in a little butter until tender and add with the sliced tomatoes to the casserole. Cover and cook for a further 20 minutes.

Chicken Hawaiian

6 chicken thighs
⅓ cup plain flour
1 teaspoon ground ginger
1 teaspoon salt
¼ teaspoon pepper
⅓ cup butter
½ cup chopped spring onion
15 oz or 425 g can crushed
   pineapple well drained
1½ teaspoons soy sauce
pineapple slices, tomato wedges
   and parsley sprigs to garnish

Remove the skin from the chicken thighs and dry each one with a paper towel. Coat the pieces with a mixture of the flour, ginger, salt and pepper. Melt the butter in a heavy-based pan, add the chicken and cook until golden. Lift out, drain on paper and place in a casserole.

To the drippings in the pan add the spring onion and brown lightly, then add the remainder of the seasoned flour. Cook, stirring until smooth and lightly coloured. Combine the syrup drained from the pineapple with the soy sauce and enough water, if necessary, to make up 1½ cups. Add to the pan and cook, stirring constantly until the gravy boils and slightly thickens.

Spoon the crushed pineapple over the chicken then add the gravy. Cover and cook in a moderate oven (350° F, 180° C) for at least 1 hour or until the chicken is tender. Serve garnished with pineapple slices, tomato wedges and parsley.

Chicken in Orange Gravy

1 medium-size roasting chicken
⅓ cup plain flour
½ teaspoon salt
½ teaspoon paprika
½ teaspoon garlic salt
3 tablespoons oil
6¾ oz or 191 g can champignons
¼ teaspoon ground nutmeg
2 teaspoons sugar
10 oz or 283 g can cream of
   mushroom soup
½ cup water
1 chicken soup cube
1 cup orange juice
2½ cups diagonally cut carrots

Cut the chicken into serving pieces. Combine the flour, salt, paprika and garlic salt and use to coat the chicken pieces. Heat the oil in a heavy-based pan and brown the chicken pieces on all sides. Lift out, drain on paper and place in a casserole.

Drain the champignons, reserving the liquid, and add them to the casserole. Sprinkle with the nutmeg and sugar.

Drain away any oil left in the pan. In a bowl blend the mushroom soup, champignon liquid, water, soup cube and orange juice. Pour into the pan and stir until boiling, scraping any browned bits from the bottom. Pour over the chicken. Cover and cook in a moderate oven (350° F, 180° C) for 25 minutes. Add the carrots, put the lid on again and replace in the oven for a further 30 minutes or until chicken and carrots are tender. Remove any fat from the surface and serve the chicken with freshly boiled rice.

Chicken in White Wine

2 roasting chickens
½ teaspoon salt
3 tablespoons plain flour
4 or 5 rashers of bacon
1 tablespoon butter
12 medium mushrooms
3 carrots scraped and sliced
   diagonally into ½-inch pieces
¼ cup chopped shallots
12 tiny white onions
1½ cups stock made from the
   chicken carcasses
½ cup white wine
1 tablespoon rice flour

Cut the chickens into serving pieces and remove most of the skin. Sprinkle each piece with salt, then dust with flour. Remove the rind and fry the bacon in a heavy-based pan until crisp. Lift out and place in a lightly greased casserole.

Brown the chicken in the bacon fat, adding the butter if necessary. As each piece is browned, drain it on paper and place with the bacon in the casserole. Sauté the mushrooms in the same pan.

Cook the carrots in boiling salted water for 5 minutes. Drain, then add with the shallots, onions, stock, wine and mushrooms to the chicken in the casserole. Cover and cook in a moderate oven (350° F, 180° C) for 1 hour or until both the chicken and the vegetables are tender.

If the gravy is too thin, blend the rice flour with a little white wine or water and add, stirring lightly. Return the casserole to the oven for another 10 minutes.

Chicken Jambalaya

2 rashers of bacon chopped
¼ cup chopped onion
2 teaspoons butter
1 tablespoon plain flour
1 cup tomato purée or pulped
   tomatoes
⅓ cup water
¼ teaspoon thyme
¼ teaspoon paprika
½ teaspoon salt
3 cups cooked rice
2 cups diced cooked chicken
½ cup chopped spring onions
2 teaspoons Worcester sauce
2 tablespoons soy sauce
hard-boiled egg slices
parsley sprigs to garnish

Sauté the diced bacon and onion in the butter in a heavy-based pan until the onion is tender. Add the flour, tomato purée, water, thyme, paprika and salt. Bring to the boil. Add the rice, cooked chicken, spring onions, Worcester sauce and soy sauce. Bring to the boil and simmer for a few minutes or until heated through. Spoon into a lightly greased casserole and top with hard-boiled egg slices and parsley sprigs, or use individual ramekins. Serve at once, or cover with greased aluminium foil and place in a slow oven (200° F, 100° C) for about 15 minutes.

Chicken Mornay with Broccoli

1 packet frozen broccoli
1 tablespoon butter
2 slightly rounded tablespoons
   plain flour
1 cup chicken broth
$\frac{1}{2}$ cup cream
$\frac{1}{2}$ cup dry white wine
salt and pepper
$\frac{1}{8}$ teaspoon Worcester sauce
grated cheese
2 cups diced cooked chicken
chopped parsley to garnish

Cook the broccoli until almost tender, drain and arrange in the bottom of a lightly greased casserole. Melt the butter in a saucepan, add the flour, stir until smooth then cook for about 2 minutes but do not allow to brown. Add the chicken broth and the cream and stir over medium heat until the sauce boils and thickens.

Stir in the wine, salt and pepper to taste, Worcester sauce and one-third of a cup of cheese. Arrange the chicken on the broccoli, pour over the sauce and sprinkle with about 2 tablespoons of grated cheese. Bake uncovered in a hot oven (425° F, 220° C) for about 15 minutes or until the sauce bubbles and the cheese browns. Sprinkle with parsley before serving.

Chicken Mornay with Broccoli

Chicken Normandy

2 medium-size roasting chickens
$\frac{1}{2}$ cup butter
$\frac{1}{4}$ cup brandy
seasoned salt and pepper
1 medium onion thinly sliced
$\frac{3}{4}$ cup thinly sliced celery
2 medium-sized tart apples
   peeled and sliced
1 tablespoon chopped parsley
$\frac{1}{4}$ teaspoon dried marjoram
$\frac{1}{3}$ cup sherry
$\frac{1}{3}$ cup cream

Cut the chicken into serving pieces and sauté them in the melted butter in a heavy-based pan until nicely browned. Transfer to a large casserole. Reserve the drippings in the pan. Heat the brandy in a small saucepan, ignite it and pour over the chicken. Sprinkle with salt and pepper.

Add the onion, celery, apple and parsley to the drippings in the frypan and cook for 3 or 4 minutes, stirring frequently. Add the marjoram and sherry and pour over the chicken in the casserole. Cover and cook in a moderate oven (350° F, 180° C) for about 1$\frac{1}{2}$ hours or until the chicken is tender. Add the cream, stir to mix well, reheat before serving.

Chicken Oceania

1 large roasting chicken
$\frac{1}{3}$ cup flour
1 teaspoon salt
$\frac{1}{2}$ teaspoon celery salt
$\frac{1}{2}$ teaspoon garlic salt
$\frac{1}{2}$ teaspoon nutmeg
$\frac{1}{4}$ cup butter
$\frac{1}{2}$ cup pineapple juice drained
   from a can of pineapple rings
1 tablespoon soy sauce
2 teaspoons sugar
pineapple rings
butter for the pineapple rings

Cut the chicken into serving pieces and coat them with a mixture of flour, salt, celery salt, garlic salt and nutmeg. Brown them in the heated butter in a heavy-based pan, drain on paper and place in a lightly greased casserole.

Combine the pineapple juice with the soy sauce and sugar and pour over the chicken in the casserole. Cover and cook in a moderate oven (350° F, 180° C) for about 1 hour or until the chicken is tender. It may be necessary to baste the chicken pieces occasionally with the juice in the casserole.

During the last 15 minutes place the pineapple rings in a single layer in an ovenproof dish and put into the oven to cook. Serve the chicken pieces topped with the sautéed pineapple rings, accompanied with rice cooked in chicken stock made from the carcass of the bird and to which a few chopped spring onions and some chopped parsley have been added.

Chicken Paprika Casserole

4 chicken portions (breasts or
   thighs)
1 rounded tablespoon plain flour

Cover the chicken portions with a mixture of flour, salt and paprika. Melt the butter in a heavy-based pan and fry the chicken until lightly

1 level teaspoon salt
1 level teaspoon paprika
1 level tablespoon butter
1 onion peeled and sliced
15 oz or 425 g can tomatoes
1 teaspoon sugar
$\frac{1}{4}$ cup sour or fresh cream
parsley to garnish

browned. Lift it out and place in a casserole.

Fry the onion in the same pan, adding a little more butter if necessary. Blend in the flour left over from coating the chicken, stir until smooth and lightly browned, then add the tomatoes (with the liquid in the can) and sugar. Stir until boiling. Pour over the chicken in the casserole. Cover and cook in a moderate oven (350° F, 180° C) for about 1 hour or until the chicken is tender. Just before serving add the cream and garnish with parsley.

Chicken Pizzaiola

1 roasting chicken (about 3 lb
    or 1.5 kg)
4 oz or 125 g butter
$\frac{1}{4}$ cup seasoned plain flour
1 clove of garlic peeled and
    chopped
2 medium onions peeled and
    finely diced
$1\frac{1}{2}$ cups stock, or water and 2
    chicken soup cubes
1 cup dry white wine
5 oz or 142 g can tomato paste
2 bay-leaves
1 tablespoon chopped parsley
salt
freshly ground pepper
1 lb or 500 g Provolone or
    Mozzarella cheese sliced

Cut the chicken into serving portions, brush each with melted butter and toss in seasoned flour. In the remaining butter sauté the garlic and onions in a heavy-based saucepan, then add the chicken and allow to brown on all sides. Stir in the remaining flour. Add the chicken stock, wine, tomato paste, bay-leaves and parsley. Season with salt and pepper to taste. Cover and simmer for 1 hour.

Transfer the chicken pieces to a shallow casserole dish and arrange cheese slices and sauce alternately over them, finishing with cheese. Cover and cook in a moderate oven (350° F, 180° C) for 30 minutes or until the cheese melts. Garnish with extra parsley if desired.

Roman Style Chicken

1 large roasting chicken
seasoned plain flour
1 tablespoon oil
1 tablespoon butter
1 medium onion
$\frac{1}{2}$ cup chopped ham
4 tablespoons dry white wine
2 or 3 ripe medium sized tomatoes
    peeled and sliced

Cut the chicken into serving pieces. Coat each with seasoned flour. Heat the oil and butter in a heavy-based pan and fry the chicken until brown on all sides. This will take about 12 minutes. Lift out and place in a casserole.

Put the onion into the pan and fry until brown. Place in the casserole and add the ham. Pour the wine into the pan and stir until boiling, then add to the casserole. Cover and cook in a moderate

54

1 green pepper seeded and cut
    into strips

oven (350° F, 180° C) for about 30 minutes. Add the tomato slices and cook for another 30 minutes. Add the pepper strips and cook for a further 15 minutes or until the chicken is tender. Check for flavouring, adding salt and pepper as required.

If you have used very watery tomatoes the liquid in the casserole may be too thin, in which case cream 2 teaspoons of butter with the same amount of plain flour and drop into the casserole, stirring lightly as it is absorbed.

Chicken Saltimbocca

8 single breasts of chicken
8 paper-thin slices of ham
8 thin pieces of Swiss cheese
$\frac{1}{4}$ cup plain flour
1 egg
1 cup fine white breadcrumbs
1 tablespoon grated Parmesan
    cheese
$\frac{1}{4}$ teaspoon garlic salt
$\frac{1}{4}$ teaspoon crumbled dry tarragon
2 tablespoons butter
$\frac{1}{2}$ cup chicken broth, or water
    and 1 soup cube
$\frac{1}{2}$ cup dry sherry
2 teaspoons cornflour blended
    with 2 teaspoons cold water

Remove any skin or bone from the chicken breasts and pound each one with a meat mallet until they are thin (be careful not to break the slices). Place a piece of ham, then a piece of cheese on each piece of chicken and roll up. Secure each with a wooden cocktail pick, dip in flour and then in lightly beaten egg, then roll each in a mixture of breadcrumbs, Parmesan cheese, garlic salt and crumbled tarragon. Sauté the rolls in the heated butter in a heavy-based pan till lightly browned, then transfer them to a shallow casserole.

Add the chicken broth and sherry to the casserole and bake uncovered at 350° F (180° C) for 30 minutes or until the chicken is tender. Lift the chicken onto a hot platter. Drain the juices into a small saucepan and bring to the boil, then stir in the blended cornflour. Keep stirring until boiling. Remove the cocktail picks and pour the sauce around the rolls before serving.

Chicken with Burgundy

1 large roasting chicken
3 oz or 90 g pork fillet
2 tablespoons butter
2 tablespoons plain flour
$15\frac{1}{4}$ oz or 432 g can Gourmet
    chicken soup
$\frac{1}{2}$ soup can water

Cut the chicken into serving pieces, discarding the skin. Cut the pork into thin slices. Heat the butter in a heavy-based pan and fry the pork until it browns lightly. Lift out. Fry the chicken pieces in the same pan. Place both in a lightly greased casserole.

With another 2 teaspoons of butter in the pan

55

4 oz or 125 g fresh mushrooms
  sliced
1 clove of garlic crushed
½ cup burgundy
6 shallots chopped

add the plain flour and stir until smooth and lightly browned, then add the chicken soup and the water. Stir until the mixture boils and lightly thickens. Return the chicken and pork to the pan and add the mushrooms, garlic, burgundy and chopped shallot. Blend well and transfer to a lightly greased casserole. Cover and cook in a moderate oven (350° F, 180° C) until the chicken is tender—about 1 hour.

Coq au Riesling

1 large roasting chicken
seasoned plain flour
1 tablespoon oil
1 tablespoon butter
dash of nutmeg
½ teaspoon dried thyme
2 or 3 spring onions cut in half
sprigs of parsley
1 small onion
2 whole cloves
⅓ cup cognac
¾ cup riesling
¾ cup water
1 chicken soup cube
2 rashers of bacon cut into 1-inch
  pieces
12 button mushrooms
12 tiny white onions
1 teaspoon sugar
pinch of salt
2 egg yolks
½ cup cream
chopped parsley to garnish

Cut the chicken into serving pieces and remove the skin. Coat each piece with seasoned flour. Heat the oil and butter in a heavy-based pan and fry the chicken pieces until brown on both sides. Sprinkle over the nutmeg, thyme, halved spring onions and parsley. Stick the cloves into the onion and add. Pour over the cognac, warm, ignite, then let the flames die down. Add the wine, water and soup cube stir until boiling, then transfer all to a lightly greased casserole. Cover and cook in a moderate oven (350° F, 180° C) for 30 to 40 minutes or until the chicken is tender.

Fry the bacon (rind removed) until crisp and add it to the casserole. Sauté the mushrooms in a little butter until tender, and add. Sauté the tiny onions in the same pan, sprinkling with the sugar and salt, then add to the casserole. Continue cooking with the lid on until the chicken and vegetables are ready to serve. Beat the egg yolks and cream together and stir into the casserole. Reheat, but do not allow to boil. Serve garnished with chopped parsley.

Coq au Vin

1 large roasting chicken
seasoned plain flour
2 tablespoons oil
2 tablespoons butter
4 rashers of bacon chopped
4 tablespoons brandy

Cut the chicken into serving pieces, toss each piece in the seasoned flour and fry until brown in a mixture of oil and butter in a heavy-based pan. Lift out and drain on paper. Remove the rind, fry the bacon lightly and leave it in the pan. Return the chicken pieces to the pan, warm the

With every Rising of the Sun, Think of your Life as just Begun.

1969

| JANUARY | FEBRUARY | MARCH | APRIL |

6 tablespoons red wine
1 bay-leaf
2 cloves
pinch of thyme
salt
freshly ground black pepper
12 tiny peeled onions
12 small button mushrooms
2 tablespoons chopped parsley

brandy, pour it over the chicken and ignite it. When the flames die down, add the red wine. Turn the mixture into a lightly greased casserole and add the bay-leaf, cloves and thyme. Season with salt and freshly ground black pepper.

If the onions are a little on the large size use half the quantity and cut into wedges. Add to the casserole. Cover and cook in a moderate oven (350° F, 180° C) for about 1 hour or until the chicken is tender. Add the button mushrooms and the parsley, cover again and replace in the oven for a further 5 or 10 minutes.

Creamy Chicken Rice Casserole

1 cup raw rice
2 tablespoons butter
¾ cup chopped onion
4 level tablespoons plain flour
1½ cups chicken stock
1 cup milk
½ cup cream
1 cup chopped mushrooms
3 cups diced cooked chicken
2 tablespoons minced parsley
1 teaspoon salt
¼ teaspoon pepper
1 teaspoon dry mustard
½ cup slivered blanched almonds

Cook the rice in boiling salted water and drain well. Melt the butter in a saucepan, add the chopped onion and sauté until tender but not brown. Add the flour and stir until smooth, then cook for 1 minute without browning. Add the chicken stock, milk and cream. Cook, stirring constantly, until the sauce boils and thickens. Simmer for 3 minutes.

Sauté the mushrooms in a little extra butter and add to the sauce, then stir in the chicken and parsley lightly. Season with the salt, pepper and mustard. Place the rice in the bottom of a lightly greased casserole, add the chicken and sprinkle the top with the almonds. Bake uncovered at 350° F (180° C) for about 30 minutes or until the sauce bubbles and the almonds brown lightly.

Creole Chicken Casserole

1 medium-size chicken
2 rounded tablespoons cornflour
1 teaspoon salt
¼ teaspoon pepper
½ teaspoon chilli powder
1 egg
soft white breadcrumbs
2 tablespoons salad oil

Cut the chicken into serving pieces and coat them with a mixture of the cornflour, salt, pepper, and chilli powder. Beat the egg, dip the chicken pieces in it, and cover with breadcrumbs.

Heat the oil in a heavy-based pan and brown the chicken well on all sides. Lift out and place in a casserole. Sprinkle over the celery. Combine the brown sugar, lemon juice and mustard and

Creole Chicken Casserole

2 stalks of celery finely chopped
2 tablespoons brown sugar
2 tablespoons lemon juice
½ level teaspoon dry mustard
For the Sauce
1 rounded tablespoon cornflour
½ level teaspoon dry mustard
1 tablespoon brown sugar
1¼ cups tomato purée
¼ cup cold water
1 chicken soup cube
¼ cup boiling water

sprinkle over the chicken.

Now make the sauce: combine the cornflour, mustard, brown sugar and tomato purée and blend with the cold water; dissolve the soup cube in the boiling water and add to the cornflour mixture. Cook over medium heat, stirring constantly until the sauce comes to the boil. Simmer for 2 minutes.

Spoon the sauce over the chicken in the casserole, cover and cook in a moderate oven (350° F, 180° C) for about 1 hour or until the chicken is tender.

Herbed Chicken

1 medium-size roasting chicken
6 oz or 185 g long-grain rice
½ teaspoon salt
¼ teaspoon pepper
⅓ cup plain flour
2 tablespoons butter or oil
½ cup sliced celery
¼ cup chopped onion
15¼ oz or 432 g can cream of
    chicken soup
¾ cup sauterne

Cook the rice in boiling salted water for 10 minutes (it will not be quite tender), then drain. Meanwhile cut the chicken into serving pieces and remove the skin. Season each piece well with salt and pepper before coating with flour. Heat the butter or oil in a heavy-based pan and brown the chicken pieces well in it.

Place the rice in the bottom of a greased casserole and arrange the chicken pieces on top. Using the pan in which the chicken was browned, sauté the celery and onion till lightly browned.

6¾ oz or 191 g can mushrooms
1 tablespoon chopped red pepper

Pour away any excess fat or oil and add the soup and sauterne, stirring till smooth. Add the mushrooms and red pepper and bring to the boil. Pour over the chicken and rice in the casserole, cover and cook in a moderate oven (350° F, 180° C) for 25 minutes. Remove the lid and replace in the oven to bake for a further 25 minutes or until the chicken is tender.

Scalloped Chicken

2 cups soft white breadcrumbs
4 tablespoons butter
1 tablespoon minced onion or
    shallot
1 teaspoon mixed herbs
¼ teaspoon salt
2 slightly rounded tablespoons
    plain flour
2 cups chicken stock, or half
    milk and half stock
½ teaspoon salt
dash of pepper
2 eggs
2 cups diced cooked chicken
parsley to garnish

Toss the breadcrumbs in 2 tablespoons heated butter in a heavy-based pan and add the onion and the herbs and ¼ teaspoon salt. Heat, stirring lightly until all the butter has been absorbed by the breadcrumbs.

For the sauce, melt the remaining 2 tablespoons butter in a saucepan, add the flour, stir until smooth, then cook for 1 minute without browning. Add the chicken stock and stir until the sauce boils and thickens. Season with ½ teaspoon salt and a dash of pepper. Add a little of this hot sauce to the lightly beaten eggs, stir until smooth, then return the mixture to the saucepan and cook, stirring constantly, until smooth. Fold in the cooked chicken.

Arrange half the buttered breadcrumbs in the bottom of a lightly greased casserole and add the chicken and sauce mixture. Top with the remaining buttered breadcrumbs. Cover and cook in a moderate oven (350° F, 180° C) for about 30 minutes. Remove the lid for the last 10 minutes to lightly brown the crumbs. Serve with a parsley garnish.

Spanish Chicken

1 large roasting chicken
1 tablespoon butter
1 tablespoon oil
1 lb 12 oz or 794 g can tomatoes
½ cup finely chopped onion
½ cup finely chopped green pepper
1 clove of garlic crushed

Cut the chicken into serving pieces and remove the skin. Heat the butter and 1 tablespoon oil in a heavy-based pan and fry the chicken on all sides until brown. Add the well-drained and roughly chopped tomatoes, the onion, green pepper, garlic, bay-leaf, cloves, oregano, salt and pepper. Simmer for 5 minutes. Turn the

1 bay-leaf
2 whole cloves
pinch of oregano
1 teaspoon salt
¼ teaspoon pepper
1 cup uncooked rice
2 tablespoons oil (for rice)
tomato juice made up to 2½ cups
　 with water
½ cup chopped red pepper
1 cup cooked green peas
parsley to garnish

mixture into a large well-greased casserole.

In the same pan cook the rice until brown in the 2 tablespoons oil. Add the 2½ cups water and tomato juice and add this rice to the chicken in the casserole. Cover and cook in a moderate oven (350° F, 180° C) for 1½ hours or until the chicken is tender and the rice cooked. Lightly fork the red pepper and peas into the chicken and rice. Cover again and cook for another 10 minutes. Discard the bay-leaf and the cloves before serving.

Casserole of Pheasant

1 pheasant
2 tablespoons butter or bacon fat
3 rashers of streaky bacon
1 onion peeled and sliced
1 carrot scraped and sliced
1 stalk of celery cut into 2-inch
　 pieces
1 bouquet garni
salt and pepper
½ glass white wine or sherry
½ cup stock, or water and 1
　 teaspoon instant stock powder

This is included with the chicken recipes for convenience, though pheasant is game, not poultry. Casseroling is one of the best methods of tenderizing pheasant, particularly if it is a little on the old side. The bird may be carved in the kitchen and served on a hot dish with the gravy in a separate bowl.

Cut off the head as close to the body as possible. Heat the butter or bacon fat in a deep saucepan or in a casserole which can take direct heat, and brown the bird all over. If it has been browned in a saucepan transfer it to a casserole. Add the bacon, prepared vegetables, bouquet garni, a sprinkle of salt and a little pepper, and the wine and stock. Cover (if the lid is difficult to keep securely on, cover instead with heavy-duty aluminium foil). Bake in a moderate oven (350° F, 180° C) for about 1½ hours or until the flesh is tender. Remove the pheasant and the bacon from the casserole and keep hot. Take out and discard the bouquet garni and strain off the vegetables. Strain the gravy, thickening it if you wish with a little blended flour, and seasoning it to taste with salt and pepper. Cut the bacon into pieces before serving it with the sliced bird, vegetables and gravy.

FISH

Alpine Tuna Casserole

15 oz or 425 g can chunk-style
    tuna
2 cups sliced celery
$\frac{1}{2}$ cup whipped salad dressing
$\frac{1}{4}$ cup chopped dried onions
$\frac{1}{2}$ teaspoon salt
pinch of pepper
4 oz or 125 g packet Swiss cheese
    slices cut into thin strips
2 tablespoons slivered toasted
    almonds

Combine all the ingredients except the almonds, mixing well. Pour into a lightly greased casserole and sprinkle with the almonds. Bake uncovered in a moderately slow oven (325° F, 160° C) for 25 to 30 minutes.

Colonial Casserole

$15\frac{1}{2}$ oz or 439 g can salmon
15 oz or 425 g can cream-style
    corn
$\frac{1}{2}$ cup unsweetened evaporated
    milk

Drain the salmon, reserving the liquid. Remove the skin and bones and flake the flesh. Place in a bowl and add the salmon liquid, corn, milk, slightly beaten eggs, salt and pepper. Turn the mixture into a lightly greased casserole. Melt

61

Colonial Casserole

2 eggs
pinch of salt
dash of pepper
1 tablespoon butter
½ cup soft white breadcrumbs
½ cup shredded processed cheese
1 tablespoon finely chopped
   chives or parsley

the butter and mix with the breadcrumbs, cheese and chives or parsley. Sprinkle on top of the salmon mixture and bake uncovered in a moderate oven (350° F, 180° C) for 25 to 30 minutes or until the top is golden.

Corn, Tuna and Potato Bake

15 oz or 425 g can tuna well
   drained
15 oz or 425 g can cream-style
   corn
2 cups mashed potato
1 tablespoon chopped onion
3 tablespoons chopped green
   pepper
dash of paprika
1 tablespoon grated Parmesan
   cheese
parsley to garnish

Place alternate layers of flaked tuna and cream-style corn in a lightly greased casserole. Combine the mashed potato with the onion, green pepper and paprika, and spread over the ingredients in the casserole. Sprinkle with the cheese and bake uncovered in a moderate oven (350° F, 180° C) for about 25 minutes or until the potato is lightly browned. Garnish with parsley.

Crab Imperial

2 small cans (6½ oz or 185 g)
   crabmeat
2 teaspoons butter
1 tablespoon plain flour
1 cup milk
1 egg
1 level teaspoon dry mustard
good pinch of cayenne
1 teaspoon seasoned salt
1 teaspoon celery salt
¼ teaspoon black pepper
2 teaspoons lemon juice
½ teaspoon Worcester sauce
4 tablespoons mayonnaise
1 tablespoon milk
paprika
parsley sprigs and tomato slices
   to garnish

Melt the butter in a saucepan, blend in the flour and cook without browning for 2 minutes. Add the milk and cook, stirring constantly, until the sauce boils and thickens. Simmer for 2 minutes then pour onto the beaten egg and add the seasonings, lemon juice, Worcester sauce and 2 tablespoons of the mayonnaise. Blend well and add the drained crabmeat, mixing lightly but thoroughly.

Turn the mixture into a greased casserole, brush with the remaining mayonnaise which has been mixed with the tablespoon of milk, and sprinkle with paprika. Bake uncovered in a moderate oven (350° F, 180° C) for about 30 minutes or until the top is bubbly and lightly browned. Serve garnished with parsley sprigs and tomato slices.

Devilled Crayfish Casserole

1½ cups freshly cooked rice
1 teaspoon grated lemon rind
1 teaspoon butter
1 rounded teaspoon plain flour
10½ oz or 298 g can cream of
   mushroom soup
2 cups fresh crayfish cooked and
   chopped
1 tablespoon lemon juice
1½ teaspoons Worcester sauce
1 teaspoon prepared mustard
good pinch cayenne pepper
butter for frying
1 cup sliced mushrooms
2 tablespoons butter
½ cup soft white breadcrumbs
½ cup grated cheese
parsley and lemon slices to
   garnish

Combine the cooked rice with the lemon rind and spread in the bottom of a lightly greased casserole. Melt the teaspoon of butter in a saucepan, add the flour, stir until smooth then cook for 1 minute without browning.

Add the mushroom soup and stir over medium heat until the mixture boils. Fold in the crayfish, lemon juice, Worcester sauce, mustard and pepper. Pour this mixture over the rice in the casserole. Melt a little butter in a frying pan and sauté the mushrooms until tender. Spoon over the crayfish mixture.

Melt the 2 tablespoons of butter in a saucepan and add the breadcrumbs, then shake over the heat until the butter has been absorbed by the breadcrumbs. Add the cheese. Spread this mixture over the layers in the casserole and bake uncovered at 400° F (200° C) for about 20 minutes or until it is thoroughly heated and the topping is brown. Serve with a parsley and lemon garnish.

Fish au Gratin with Mushroom Sherry Sauce

1½ lb or 750 g fish fillets
salt and pepper
½ cup chopped parsley
1 tablespoon butter
1 tablespoon lemon juice
½ lb or 250 g cultivated
  mushrooms sliced
1½ slightly rounded tablespoons
  plain flour
1 cup milk
½ cup cream
1 tablespoon sherry
2 teaspoons soft white
  breadcrumbs
2 teaspoons grated Parmesan
  cheese
parsley and lemon slices to
  garnish

Season the fish fillets with salt and pepper and place in a lightly greased casserole dish. Sprinkle over the chopped parsley.

In a saucepan melt the butter and add the lemon juice and mushrooms. Sauté for about 5 minutes. Blend in the flour, cook for 1 minute, then add the milk and cream and stir until the sauce boils and thickens. Add the sherry, ¼ teaspoon salt and a dash of pepper. Spoon this sauce over the fish fillets and top with the mixture of breadcrumbs and cheese. Bake uncovered in a moderate oven (350° F, 180° C) for about 30 minutes. Serve with a parsley and lemon garnish.

Fish Bon Femme

2 lb or 1 kg fresh or frozen fish
  fillets
2 slices lemon
sprig of parsley
few peppercorns
3 tablespoons white wine
½ cup water
4 oz or 125 g butter
3 tablespoons chopped shallots
8 oz or 250 g cultivated
  mushrooms sliced
salt and pepper
2 tablespoons plain flour
½ cup milk and ½ cup cream, or
  1 cup milk
3 tablespoons grated cheese
1 tablespoon chopped parsley
½ cup buttered breadcrumbs

Place the fish fillets in a lightly greased casserole and add the lemon, parsley, peppercorns and wine. Add about ½ cup of water, cover and bake in a moderate oven (350° F, 180° C) for about 30 minutes or until the flesh of the fish can be easily flaked with a fork. Drain, reserving the liquid, and replace the fish in the casserole.

Melt 2 ounces of the butter in a saucepan and add the shallots and mushrooms. Sauté until both are tender, then season with salt and pepper. Spread over the fish in the casserole.

Melt the remaining 2 ounces of butter in the same saucepan, add the flour, stir until smooth, then cook for 2 minutes without browning. Measure the liquid saved from cooking the fish and make it up to ¾ cup with water or wine. Add with the milk and cream, and cook, stirring constantly, until the sauce boils and thickens. Stir in the cheese and parsley and season to taste with salt and pepper. Pour over the fish in the casserole and sprinkle with the buttered bread-

64

crumbs. Bake uncovered in a moderate oven (350° F, 180° C) for about 30 minutes or until the sauce bubbles and the crumbs brown.

Italian Cod Casserole

1 lb or 500 g smoked cod
cayenne pepper
1 tablespoon butter
½ red pepper finely chopped
½ green pepper finely chopped
2 firm tomatoes peeled and
  sliced
1 small clove of garlic crushed
1 tablespoon grated cheese
chopped parsley to garnish

Soak the cod in tepid water for about 15 minutes. Drain well. Place in a saucepan, cover with cold water and bring slowly to the boil. Simmer for 5 minutes. Drain and flake lightly. Place in the bottom of a lightly greased casserole and sprinkle lightly with cayenne pepper.

Heat the butter in a saucepan, add the chopped peppers and sauté until soft but not brown. Add the tomato slices and the garlic. Cook for about 5 minutes. Arrange over the cod and sprinkle with the grated cheese. Bake uncovered at 350° F (180° C) for about 20 minutes or until the cheese melts and lightly browns. Serve sprinkled with chopped parsley.

Layered Salmon Casserole

1 tablespoon butter
1 tablespoon plain flour
15½ oz or 439 g can cream of
  asparagus soup
8 oz or 227 g can salmon
1 teaspoon chopped parsley
squeeze of lemon juice
2 cups freshly cooked rice
buttered breadcrumbs

Melt the butter in a saucepan and stir in the flour. Cook until smooth, but do not allow the mixture to brown. Add the asparagus soup and stir until the mixture boils and thickens.

Drain and flake the salmon and stir lightly into the sauce, then add the parsley and the lemon juice. Alternate layers of cooked rice and the salmon-asparagus mixture in a lightly greased casserole. The top layer should be salmon. Sprinkle the top with the buttered breadcrumbs and bake uncovered in a moderate oven (350° F, 180° C) until the sauce bubbles and the crumbs brown—about 20 minutes.

Salmon and Vegetable Medley

2 tablespoons butter
3 tablespoons plain flour
1½ cups milk
pinch of mustard
salt and pepper

Melt the butter in a saucepan, add the flour, stir until smooth then cook for 2 minutes without browning. Add the milk and stir until the sauce boils and thickens. Season with the mustard and salt and pepper to taste.

65

8 oz or 227 g can salmon drained
and flaked
15½ oz or 439 g can whole kernel
corn
1 packet frozen peas cooked
1 tablespoon chopped shallot
2 rashers of bacon diced
slices of bread
butter
grated cheese
tomato wedges and parsley
sprigs to garnish

Toss the flaked salmon in a bowl with the corn, peas, chopped shallot and diced bacon. Stir the sauce in, taste and add more salt and pepper if necessary and turn into a lightly greased casserole.

Toast 2 slices of bread on one side only. Spread the untoasted side with butter and sprinkle thickly with grated cheese. Cut into fingers and arrange them on top of the ingredients in the casserole. Bake uncovered in a moderate oven (350° F, 180° C) for about 30 minutes or until the sauce bubbles and the cheese melts and lightly browns. Serve with fresh tomato wedges and sprigs of parsley to garnish.

Salmon Casserole 1

15½ oz or 439 g can salmon
1 cup cooked rice
1 cup sliced mushrooms
3 tablespoons butter
2 or 3 spring onions
2 rounded tablespoons plain flour
milk and the liquid from the
salmon
lemon juice
salt and pepper
2 teaspoons chopped parsley
1 tablespoon grated cheese

Drain the salmon, reserving the liquid and flake the flesh.

Place the rice in the bottom of a lightly greased casserole. Sauté the mushrooms in 1 tablespoon of the butter and spread over the rice.

Melt the other 2 tablespoons of butter in a saucepan and add the chopped spring onions. Sauté until soft. Add the flour, stir until smooth, then cook for 2 minutes without browning. Add enough milk to the salmon liquid to make 2 cups, add to the saucepan and stir until the sauce boils and thickens. Simmer for 2 minutes, then add the lemon juice, salt and pepper to taste and the chopped parsley.

Fold in the flaked salmon and spread over the mushrooms in the casserole. Top with the grated cheese. Cover and cook in a moderate oven (350° F, 180° C) for about 20 minutes or until the cheese melts and the sauce bubbles.

Salmon Casserole 2

15½ oz or 439 g can flaked salmon
2 cups cooked and well drained
rice
½ cup grated tasty cheese

Combine the drained and lightly flaked salmon, rice, cheese, milk, soup and onion in a bowl. Mix lightly, then place in a lightly greased casserole.

66

½ cup unsweetened canned milk

15 oz or 425 g can cream of mushroom soup

2 to 4 tablespoons finely chopped onion

¾ cup slightly crushed cornflakes

3 tablespoons butter melted

hot buttered asparagus

2 teaspoons chopped parsley

Mix the cornflakes with the melted butter and sprinkle over the salmon mixture. Bake uncovered in a moderate oven (350° F, 180° C) for about 30 minutes or until thoroughly heated. Top with well-drained asparagus spears and fill the centre with the chopped parsley. Serve with the extra asparagus.

Cooked chicken or tuna may replace the salmon.

Salmon Curry Creme

15½ oz or 439 g can salmon

1 large onion peeled and diced

2 tablespoons butter

2 tablespoons plain flour

2 teaspoons curry powder

salt and pepper

⅓ cup water

1⅔ cups unsweetened canned milk

3 hard-boiled eggs peeled and sliced

½ cup grated cheese

paprika

Drain, bone and lightly flake the salmon. Put the onion and butter into a saucepan and cook until the onion is tender but not brown. Add the flour, stir until smooth, then cook for 1 minute without browning. Add the curry powder and some salt and pepper to taste.

Combine the water with the milk and add to the saucepan, stir until the sauce boils and thickens. Fold in the sliced eggs and the flaked salmon. Turn the mixture into a lightly greased casserole. Sprinkle the top with the cheese and some paprika and bake uncovered in a moderate oven (350° F, 180° C) for 15 to 20 minutes. Serve with buttered rice tossed with well-drained kernel-style corn and cooked or frozen peas.

Salmon Rice Medley

15½ oz or 439 g can salmon

2 tablespoons butter

2 unpeeled red apples diced

1 cup diced celery

½ cup diced onion

10½ oz or 298 g can vegetable soup

1 cup milk

2 cups cooked rice

1 tablespoon butter melted

1 cup crushed potato crisps

½ level teaspoon curry powder

parsley to garnish

Drain, bone and lightly flake the salmon. In a large saucepan melt 2 tablespoons butter and add the diced apple, celery and onion. Sauté until tender but not brown. Add the soup, then gradually stir in the milk.

Add the flaked salmon and the cooked rice. Turn the mixture into a lightly greased casserole. Combine the melted butter with the potato crisps and curry powder and sprinkle on top of the casserole. Bake uncovered at 350° F (180° C) for about 30 minutes or until heated through and lightly browned on top. Serve garnished with parsley.

Seafood Corn Casserole

15½ oz or 439 g can salmon
3 eggs
15½ oz or 439 g can cream-style
  corn
½ cup milk
¼ teaspoon Tabasco
½ teaspoon salt
½ teaspoon dry mustard
½ teaspoon Worcester sauce
3 teaspoons lemon juice
1 cup buttered breadcrumbs
1 tablespoon grated Parmesan
  cheese
lemon and parsley to garnish

Drain, bone and flake the salmon. Beat the eggs slightly and add the corn and milk. Season with the Tabasco, salt, mustard, Worcester sauce and lemon juice. Mix well, then fold in the prepared salmon. Turn the mixture into a lightly greased casserole and sprinkle the top with the breadcrumbs and cheese. Bake uncovered in a moderate oven (350° F, 180° C) for about 30 minutes or until it is set and the top is lightly browned. Serve with a lemon and parsley garnish.

Serbian Fish

6 whiting fillets
2 rashers of bacon
2 teaspoons plain flour
1 teaspoon paprika
2 medium potatoes, peeled,
  sliced ½ inch thick and
  parboiled
1 medium onion peeled and
  thinly sliced
2 medium tomatoes peeled and
  thickly sliced
salt and paprika
1 tablespoon butter
½ cup cultured sour cream
parsley to garnish

Skin the fish fillets and place a small piece of bacon on each. Fold the fish over the bacon. Combine the flour and paprika and use this mixture to coat the fish.

In a lightly greased casserole place the parboiled potatoes, cover with the sliced onion and then the tomato slices, sprinkling lightly with salt and paprika.

Arrange the fish on top of the vegetables in the casserole and dot with butter. Cover with the casserole lid or with greased foil and cook for about 15 minutes in a moderate oven (350° F, 180° C). Remove the cover and pour over the sour cream. Return the casserole to the oven and bake uncovered for a further 15 minutes or until the fish is tender and the vegetables cooked. Serve with a parsley garnish.

Seven Seas Casserole

15½ oz or 439 g can salmon
10½ oz or 298 g can cream of
  mushroom soup
1⅔ cups unsweetened canned
  milk

Drain, bone and flake the salmon. Combine the soup, milk and salt in a saucepan and stir until boiling. Pour half into a lightly greased casserole. Now add layers of rice, flaked salmon and peas.

At this stage you could sprinkle with a little

¼ teaspoon salt
1 cup cooked rice
1 cup cooked or frozen peas
cheese slices

pepper or paprika. Pour over the remaining soup mixture and top with cheese. If you are using paprika, sprinkle a little over the cheese. Bake uncovered in a moderately hot oven (375° F, 190° C) for 30 or 40 minutes or until the cheese has melted and is lightly browned.

For additional flavour add ¼ cup finely chopped shallots and 1 teaspoon lemon juice to the soup mixture.

Smoked Cod and Rice Casserole

1 lb or 500 g smoked cod
⅓ cup raw rice
3 tablespoons butter or margarine
3 tablespoons plain flour
2 cups milk
¾ teaspoon salt
¼ teaspoon pepper
pinch of cayenne pepper
1 teaspoon lemon juice
1 tablespoon chopped parsley
3 tablespoons soft white
    breadcrumbs
3 tablespoons grated cheese
tomato wedges and parsley sprigs
    to garnish

Wash the cod, place it in a saucepan with cold water, bring to the boil, then drain. Cover with fresh water, bring to the boil again and simmer until tender. This will take about 10 minutes. Drain, remove any skin and bones and flake the flesh. Wash the rice and cook it in boiling salted water until tender. Drain well.

Melt the butter in a saucepan and stir in the flour. Cook, stirring well for about 2 minutes, then add the milk, salt, pepper and cayenne. Stir over medium heat until the sauce boils and thickens. Simmer for 3 minutes, then add the lemon juice and parsley.

Combine the sauce with the flaked cod and cooked rice and turn into a lightly greased casserole. Sprinkle the top thickly with the breadcrumbs and cheese and bake uncovered in a moderate oven (350° F, 180° C) for about 30 minutes. Top with tomato wedges and garnish with parsley.

Soused Fish

2 lb or 1 kg fish fillets
¾ cup white wine vinegar
¾ cup boiling water
2 cloves
1 bay-leaf
4 peppercorns
1 small clove of garlic
2 or 3 sprigs parsley

Roll up the fillets and stand them upright in a lightly greased casserole. Combine the remaining ingredients in a saucepan and bring to the boil. Pour this hot liquid over the fish. Cover and cook in a moderate oven (350° F, 180° C) for about 20 minutes or until the flesh can be flaked lightly with a fork (the time will depend on the thickness of the fish). Remove the casserole from the oven,

3 slices onion or 2 tablespoons
  chopped shallot
¾ teaspoon salt
pinch of cayenne pepper

take off the lid and allow to become quite cold. To keep the fish moist and improve the flavour, baste occasionally with the liquid in which it was cooked.

When cold lift out with a slotted spoon onto a serving platter. Serve with salad vegetables and, if liked, with sauce tartare.

Tuna Casserole with Cheese Whirls

7½ oz or 213 g can tuna
3 tablespoons chopped onion
⅓ cup chopped green pepper
  (optional)
3 tablespoons butter
1 teaspoon salt
6 tablespoons plain flour
1½ to 2 cups unsweetened canned
  milk
15 oz or 425 g can condensed
  chicken soup
1 tablespoon lemon juice
For the cheese whirls
2 cups self-raising flour
pinch of salt
1 tablespoon butter
½ cup unsweetened canned milk
½ cup water
melted butter
grated cheese

Drain and flake the tuna. Sauté the onion and green pepper in the butter until the onion is golden, add the salt and flour and stir with a wooden spoon until the mixture is smooth. Add the canned milk and the chicken soup and stir until boiling. Simmer for 2 minutes, stirring constantly, then add the tuna and the lemon juice. Pour into a lightly greased casserole and top with the cheese whirls.

To make the cheese whirls, first sift the flour and salt into a bowl, rub in the butter, mix to a soft dough with the milk and water and turn onto a floured board. Knead lightly, roll into an oblong approximately ¼ inch thick, brush with melted butter and sprinkle with cheese. Roll up like a Swiss roll. Cut into ½-inch slices and place cut side down on top of the casserole. Bake uncovered in a moderately hot oven (375° F, 190° C) for about 30 minutes.

Tuna Rice Casserole

15 oz or 425 g can tuna
¾ cup rice
water or stock
1 teaspoon salt
2 tablespoons butter
1 tablespoon grated onion
1 tablespoon chopped red pepper
2 tablespoons plain flour
2 cups unsweetened canned milk

Drain and flake the tuna. Wash the rice, place in a saucepan, add plenty of cold water, then the salt and the stock (or a mixture of water and either a soup cube or some instant stock powder). Bring to the boil and cook until the rice is tender. Drain, then run hot water through to separate the grains.

Melt the butter in a medium-sized saucepan and add the onion and red pepper. Sauté for

salt and pepper
$\frac{1}{2}$ teaspoon made mustard
$\frac{1}{2}$ cup crushed potato crisps

about 5 minutes but do not allow to brown. Add the flour, stir until smooth then cook for about 2 minutes. Add the milk and stir until the sauce boils and thickens, then season to taste with salt and pepper and add the mustard.

Arrange half the rice in a lightly greased casserole, cover with half the flaked tuna then half the sauce. Repeat the layers. Sprinkle with the crushed potato crisps and bake uncovered in a moderate oven (350° F, 180° C) for 20 to 30 minutes.

Tuna Medley

$7\frac{3}{4}$ oz or 220 g can tuna or salmon
2 cups cooked egg noodles or macaroni
2 tablespoons butter or margarine
$\frac{1}{4}$ cup chopped spring onions
3 slightly rounded tablespoons plain flour
$\frac{1}{4}$ teaspoon celery salt
dash of pepper
1 large can undiluted evaporated milk
$\frac{3}{4}$ cup water
$\frac{1}{4}$ cup stuffed olives
paprika

Drain and flake the tuna. Have the noodles cooked and well drained. Melt the butter in a saucepan, add the spring onions and sauté until tender but not brown. Blend in the flour, celery salt, and pepper. Cook without browning for 1 minute, then add the milk and water and stir until the sauce boils and thickens. Fold in the tuna and the chopped olives.

Arrange the noodles in the bottom of a lightly greased casserole and pour over the sauce mixture. Toss lightly with a fork to blend. Sprinkle with paprika. Bake uncovered at 350° F (180° C) for about 30 minutes.

If liked, the casserole may be topped with $\frac{1}{2}$ cup grated cheese, then replaced in the oven to melt and lightly brown the cheese.

Tuna Ramekins

$7\frac{1}{2}$ oz or 213 g can tuna
$1\frac{1}{2}$ cups cooked rice
1 tablespoon butter
1 tablespoon chopped onion
1 tablespoon chopped red pepper
1 tablespoon chopped green pepper
$1\frac{1}{4}$ cups medium thick white sauce
salt and pepper
mustard
lemon juice

Drain and flake the tuna. Have the rice freshly cooked and well drained. Melt the butter in a saucepan, add the onion and the red and green peppers and sauté until soft but not brown. Add the rice and toss lightly to blend.

Divide the mixture evenly between 6 lightly greased ramekins (or use one casserole). Spread the flaked fish over the rice.

Flavour the white sauce with salt, pepper, a little mustard and lemon juice and spoon over the fish. Top with the grated cheese. Bake uncovered in a moderate oven (350° F, 180° C) for about

½ cup grated cheese
lemon and parsley to garnish

20 minutes to thoroughly heat the mixture and to melt and lightly brown the cheese. Serve with a lemon and parsley garnish.

Tuna Tomato Bake

7½ oz or 213 g can tuna
1 packet mushroom soup mix
1½ cups water
1⅔ cups unsweetened canned milk
6 oz or 185 g cooked spaghetti
2 tablespoons sliced stuffed olives
1 cup coarsely grated or diced cheese
1 medium tomato peeled and quartered
¼ cup finely grated Cheddar or Parmesan cheese
tomato slices to garnish

Drain and lightly flake the fish. Put the soup mix into a saucepan, add the water and stir over medium heat until thoroughly blended. Add the milk and stir until boiling.

Combine the sauce with the cooked spaghetti, sliced olives, coarsely grated or diced cheese, flaked fish and quartered tomato. Turn the mixture into a lightly greased casserole and sprinkle the top with the finely grated cheese. Bake uncovered in a moderate oven (350° F, 180° C) for 25 or 30 minutes or until heated through and golden brown in colour. Garnish with tomato slices.

Salmon may be used instead of tuna if preferred.

Tuna Ramekins

LAMB

Braised Lamb Chops

4 shoulder lamb chops
seasoned plain flour
2 tablespoons butter or fat
1 large onion peeled and sliced
$\frac{2}{3}$ cup white wine
4 tablespoons stock
4 medium potatoes
1 cup sliced mushrooms
1 teaspoon salt
1 small packet frozen peas

Trim the chops of excess fat and coat them with seasoned flour. Heat the butter in a heavy-based pan and brown the chops on both sides. Lift out and place in a casserole.

Add the onion to the fat left in the pan and cook until it browns. Add the wine and stock. Cook, stirring constantly, until the mixture boils and slightly thickens. Pour over the chops in the casserole. Cover and cook in a moderate oven (350° F, 180° C) for about 45 minutes.

Meanwhile peel the potatoes and cook them in boiling salted water until almost soft. Drain, cut into cubes and add to the casserole together with the mushrooms, enough salt to flavour, and the peas. Cover again and return the casserole to the oven to cook for a further 30 or 40 minutes.

◀ *Tuna Medley*
◀ *Seven Seas Casserole*

Curried Chop Casserole

6 thick chump chops
1 rounded tablespoon plain flour
1 teaspoon salt
1 green apple peeled and chopped
1 banana peeled and sliced
1 tomato peeled and sliced
1 tablespoon oil
1 onion peeled and chopped
$\frac{1}{2}$ to 1 tablespoon curry powder
squeeze of lemon juice
$\frac{3}{4}$ pint water
1 soup cube, or 2 teaspoons
   instant onion stock powder
1 bay-leaf

Trim the chops, removing as much fat as possible, then toss them in the flour and salt. Prepare the apple, banana and tomato.

Heat the oil in a pan and fry the chops lightly on both sides. Lift out, drain on paper and place in a casserole. Add the onion to the pan and cook, stirring constantly, until golden. Lift out and add to the casserole.

Add a little more oil to the pan if necessary and add the remainder of the flour and the curry powder. Cook, stirring well, until the mixture bubbles. Add the water and the soup cube and stir until boiling. Pour this mixture over the chops and add the apple, banana, tomato, lemon juice and bay-leaf. Cover and cook in a moderate oven (350° F, 180° C) for about 2 hours. Remove the bay-leaf and serve the curry with freshly boiled rice.

The dish may be accompanied with coconut, peanuts, chutney or other curry condiments.

Dilled Lamb Casserole

2 lb or 1 kg boneless lamb cut
   into 1-inch cubes
2 tablespoons oil
1 teaspoon salt
$\frac{1}{2}$ teaspoon dried dill
$1\frac{1}{2}$ tablespoons plain flour
$1\frac{1}{2}$ cups water or stock
2 cups sliced carrots
$1\frac{1}{2}$ cups sliced celery
2 tablespoons chopped shallots
$\frac{1}{2}$ cup cultured sour cream
1 tablespoon chopped parsley to
   garnish

Heat the oil in a heavy-based pan. Toss the lamb cubes in a mixture of salt, dill and flour, add to the pan and cook until brown on all sides. Lift out with a slotted spoon and place in a lightly greased casserole.

To the oil left in the pan add any flour left over from coating the lamb, cook until smooth and brown and then add the stock or water and stir until the gravy boils and slightly thickens. Pour over the lamb in the casserole and add the carrots, celery and shallots. Cover and cook in a moderate oven (350° F, 180° C) for about 2 hours.

Just before serving add the cultured cream, reheat without boiling and serve topped with the chopped parsley.

Family Casserole

6 leg lamb chops
seasoned plain flour
1 to 2 tablespoons fat
1 onion peeled and finely
  chopped
1½ cups water
1 clove of garlic crushed
  (optional)
2 teaspoons salt
good pinch of pepper
2 medium carrots peeled and
  sliced
3 medium potatoes peeled and
  sliced
1½ cups frozen peas
chopped parsley to garnish

Remove any surplus fat from the chops, then cut the flesh from the bones and cut it into 1-inch pieces. Toss the pieces in seasoned flour. Heat the fat in a pan and fry the meat lightly on both sides. Lift out, drain and place in a casserole.

Add the chopped onion to the pan and cook until brown, stirring in about 1 tablespoon flour. Add the water and stir until boiling. Now add the garlic, salt and pepper and pour over the meat in the casserole. Cover and cook in a moderate oven (350° F, 180° C) for 1½ hours. Now add the carrots and potatoes and cook for a further 40 minutes with the lid on. Add the frozen peas and return the casserole to the oven for another 10 minutes. Serve sprinkled with chopped parsley.

French Lamb Casserole

1½ tablespoons oil
2 lb or 1 kg lean lamb cut into
  1-inch cubes
1 medium onion peeled and
  chopped
1 clove of garlic crushed
1 slightly rounded tablespoon
  plain flour
1½ teaspoons salt
good pinch of pepper
¼ teaspoon marjoram
1 small bay-leaf
1½ cups chicken stock, or water
  and 1 chicken soup cube
1 tablespoon lemon juice or
  white wine
8 tiny white onions
3 small carrots scraped and
  sliced
3 medium potatoes peeled and
  quartered
1 teaspoon chopped parsley to
  garnish

Heat the oil in a heavy-based pan, add the lamb cubes and cook until lightly browned on all sides. Lift out with a slotted spoon and place in a lightly greased casserole.

Add the onions to the oil left in the pan (add a little more oil if necessary). Cook, stirring constantly, until a golden colour. Add the garlic and then the flour. Stir until smooth and cook until brown. Season with the salt, pepper and marjoram and add the bay-leaf, chicken stock and lemon juice. Stir until the mixture boils and slightly thickens, then pour over the lamb in the casserole. Add the prepared onions, carrots and potatoes, cover and cook in a moderate oven (350° F, 180° C) for about 2 hours or until both the meat and vegetables are tender. Serve sprinkled with the chopped parsley.

Indian Lamb Curry

2 lb or 1 kg lean lamb cubed
¼ cup plain flour
1½ tablespoons butter
½ cup finely minced onion
2 teaspoons salt
¼ teaspoon monosodium
  glutamate
¼ teaspoon dry mustard
1 to 2 tablespoons curry powder
1 teaspoon sugar
1 cup water
1 tablespoon lemon juice
1 tart apple peeled and diced
1 tablespoon flaked coconut
1 tablespoon raisins
dash of nutmeg

Toss the cubed lamb in the flour and brown in the hot butter. Add the minced onion and sauté until soft, then add the remaining ingredients, mixing well. Bring to simmering point and transfer to a casserole. Cover and cook in a moderate oven (350° F, 180° C) for about 2 hours or until the meat is tender but not ragged. Serve with freshly boiled rice and your favourite curry condiments.

Irish Casserole

1½ lb or 750 g forequarter or
  best end neck chops
seasoned plain flour
2 onions peeled and sliced
2 stalks of celery (with leaves)
  finely chopped
2 carrots scraped and sliced
1 tablespoon chopped parsley
1 teaspoon salt
dash of pepper
3 medium potatoes peeled and
  cut into thick slices
1¼ cups water
1 soup cube
chopped parsley to garnish

Remove any excess fat from the chops and coat them with seasoned flour. Lightly grease a casserole and place half the sliced onion in the bottom. Cover with half the celery, carrot and parsley then top with the coated chops. Cover with the remaining parsley, carrot, celery and onion in that order (the last layer should be onion), seasoning each layer lightly with salt and pepper. Now top with the potato slices and pour over the water and the crumbled soup cube. Cover and cook in a moderate oven (350° F, 180° C) for about 2 hours or until the chops and the vegetables are tender. Garnish with chopped parsley.

Lamb and Mushroom Casserole

4 thick leg lamb chops
2 tablespoons seasoned plain flour
1 tablespoon butter
4 oz or 125 g cultivated
  mushrooms sliced

Trim the chops of excess fat, then coat them with the seasoned flour. Melt the butter in a pan and brown the chops on both sides. Lift out, drain on paper and place in a lightly greased casserole.
Sprinkle any remaining flour into the pan

1 tablespoon lemon juice
4 small white onions
1 bay-leaf
$\frac{3}{4}$ cup peas
1 tablespoon dry sherry
$\frac{3}{4}$ cup stock

and cook, stirring constantly, until brown. Now add the remaining ingredients and stir until boiling. Pour over the chops in the casserole and season to taste with salt and pepper. Cover and cook in a moderate oven (350° F, 180° C) for 1½ hours or until the chops are tender.

Lamb and Onion Casserole

6 chump chops
1 rounded tablespoon plain flour
butter for frying
4 rashers of bacon
12 tiny or 2 medium-sized
    (chopped) white onions
2 medium carrots scraped and
    sliced
4 oz or 125 g cultivated
    mushrooms peeled and
    quartered
1¼ cups boiling water
1 beef soup cube or 2 teaspoons
    instant stock powder

Trim the chops of excess fat and coat them with flour. Fry quickly in the heated butter in a heavy-based pan until brown on both sides. Lift out and place in a casserole. Remove the rind and chop the bacon, then add it to the pan together with the onions, sliced carrots and mushroom quarters. Cook for 3 or 4 minutes, then pour over the chops in the casserole.

Stir any remaining flour into the pan and cook until brown. Add the water and the crumbled soup cube and stir until boiling. Add to the casserole. Cover and cook in a moderate oven (350° F, 180° C) for 1¾ hours or until the chops are tender.

Lamb Casserole

2 lb or 1 kg boneless lamb cut
    into 1-inch cubes
½ teaspoon sugar
1 tablespoon butter or oil
2 teaspoons salt
¼ teaspoon pepper
¼ cup plain flour
1½ cups water
1 beef soup cube or 2 teaspoons
    instant stock powder
½ cup red wine
1 teaspoon Worcester sauce
1 clove of garlic crushed
6 small carrots scraped and diced
4 small white onions quartered
4 stalks celery chopped
4 medium potatoes sliced or cubed
parsley to garnish

Sprinkle the lamb with the sugar, and brown on all sides in the heated butter or oil. Stir in the salt, pepper and flour and cook for 2 minutes, then add the water, crumbled soup cube, wine, sauce and garlic. Stir until boiling, then transfer to a casserole. Cover and cook in a moderate oven (350° F, 180° C) for about 1½ hours.

Add the vegetables, return the covered casserole to the oven and cook for a further 45 minutes or until both the meat and the vegetables are tender. Serve with a parsley garnish.

Lamb Chop and Vegetable Casserole

4 thick lamb shoulder or chump
    chops
1 teaspoon salt
freshly ground black pepper
pinch of thyme
1 tablespoon butter or fat
2 onions peeled and sliced
1 clove of garlic crushed
1 cup water
1 chicken soup cube
4 small potatoes peeled and
    sliced
1 green pepper seeded and sliced
2 medium tomatoes peeled and
    sliced
1 small bay-leaf crumbled

Sprinkle the chops with a little salt, black pepper and thyme. Melt the butter or fat in a large heavy-based pan and fry the chops for about 2 minutes on both sides. Lift out and drain on paper. Fry the onion in the pan until golden (if necessary add a little more butter). Lift out with a slotted spoon and set aside. Pour the water and crumble the soup cube into the pan and bring to the boil, scraping any brown bits from the bottom of the pan.

Spread half the onion and half the garlic in the bottom of a lightly greased casserole, cover with the potato slices, the sliced green pepper and half the tomato slices. Season again with salt, pepper and thyme to taste, and add the bay-leaf. Add another layer of the onion and garlic and the remaining tomato slices. Pour over the gravy. Arrange the chops on top, cover and cook in a moderate oven (350° F, 180° C) for about 40 minutes or until the chops are tender.

Lamb Chop Curry

6 shoulder lamb chops
½ cup seasoned plain flour
2 tablespoons butter or margarine
3 small onions peeled and
    chopped
1 clove of garlic peeled and
    crushed
3 teaspoons curry powder (or
    more according to taste)
1½ tablespoons plain flour
1½ tablespoons chutney
2 medium tomatoes peeled and
    diced
2 small bananas peeled and sliced
1 teaspoon salt
pinch of allspice

Trim the excess fat from the chops before coating with seasoned flour. Heat the butter or margarine in a heavy-based pan and brown the chops on both sides. Lift out, drain on paper and place in a casserole.

Add the onion to the drippings left in the pan and fry until brown, then stir in the garlic. Add 1½ tablespoons of flour (it could be some left over from coating the chops) and the curry powder. Cook, stirring constantly for about 2 minutes. Add the chutney, tomato, sliced bananas, salt and allspice, then the stock and lemon juice. Cook, stirring constantly, until the liquid boils and thickens slightly.

Pour this curry gravy over the chops, cover and cook in a moderate oven (350° F, 180° C)

78

1 cup stock, or water and 1 soup
   cube or 1 teaspoon instant
   stock powder
1½ teaspoons lemon juice

for about 1½ hours or until the chops are tender.
Serve with freshly boiled rice and your favourite
curry accompaniments.

Lancashire Casserole

8 thick shoulder chops
butter or oil
2 large onions peeled and
   chopped
2 carrots peeled and chopped
1½ tablespoons butter
1½ tablespoons plain flour
1½ cups water
2 beef soup cubes
pinch of thyme
1 teaspoon salt
dash of pepper
1 teaspoon Worcester sauce
1½ tablespoons sherry
4 medium potatoes peeled and
   sliced

Trim the chops of any excess fat and brown them
lightly in a little butter in a heavy-based pan.
Lift out, drain on paper and place in a casserole.
Add the peeled and chopped onions and carrots
to the drippings left in the pan, sauté until
golden, then spoon over the chops.

Make up enough butter in the pan to equal
about 1½ tablespoons, blend in the flour and stir
until brown. Add the water, the crumbled soup
cubes, thyme, salt, pepper, Worcester sauce and
sherry and stir until boiling. Pour over the
ingredients in the casserole. Top with the potato
slices, overlapping them slightly. Cover and cook
in a moderate oven (350° F, 180° C) for about
2 hours or until the meat and potatoes are tender.
Remove the lid from the casserole and bake for a
further 10 minutes to brown the potatoes lightly.

Lemon Pepper Lamb Chops

6 thick lamb chops
2 tablespoons seasoned plain
   flour
2 tablespoons fat
1 large onion peeled and cut
   into 6 slices
1 large lemon cut into 6 slices
1 green pepper cut into 6 rings
1½ cups tomato juice

Trim the chops of any excess fat and coat them
with the seasoned flour. Heat the fat in a heavy-
based pan and brown the chops on both sides.
Lift out, drain on paper to absorb any fat and
place in a casserole.

On top of each chop place a slice of onion,
one of lemon and one of green pepper. Now
pour the tomato juice over all. Cover and cook
in a moderate oven (350° F, 180° C) for about
1½ hours or until the chops are tender.

Marinated Lamb Chops

⅔ cup dry white wine
1½ tablespoons wine vinegar
2 teaspoons brown sugar
1 small clove of garlic crushed
6 lamb shoulder chops
1 tablespoon butter
½ cup stock
1 teaspoon chilli sauce
1 teaspoon salt
1 tablespoon finely chopped
   onion
2 teaspoons cornflour

Combine the wine, vinegar, brown sugar and garlic and pour over the chops in a shallow casserole. Marinate for several hours, turning once or twice. Drain the chops, reserving the marinade. Melt the butter in a large pan and brown the chops on both sides. Lift out and place in a casserole.

Using the pan in which the chops were browned, heat the reserved marinade with the stock, chilli sauce, salt and onion, stirring until boiling. Pour over the chops in the casserole, cover and cook in a moderate oven (350° F, 180° C) for 1½ hours or until the chops are tender. Blend the cornflour with a little water and add to the casserole. Cover and replace in the oven to cook for another 10 minutes.

Spanish Lamb

½ cup finely chopped onion
1 clove of garlic minced
1 tablespoon salad oil or butter
1 lb or 500 g ripe tomatoes
   skinned and chopped
¾ cup tomato purée
⅓ cup water
1 bay-leaf
2 cups diced cooked lamb
¼ cup sliced stuffed olives
½ lb or 250 g cooked spaghetti
grated Parmesan cheese for
   topping

Sauté the onion and garlic in the hot oil or butter until tender but not brown. Stir in the tomatoes and the tomato purée, the water and the bay-leaf. Transfer to a lightly greased casserole, cover and cook in a moderate oven (350° F, 180° C) stirring occasionally. Now add the lamb and the olives. Cook for another 10 minutes, then remove the bay-leaf.

Cook the spaghetti in the usual way, and drain well. Pour the meat mixture over the spaghetti and sprinkle the top with grated Parmesan cheese.

Spanish Lamb Chops

2 lb or 1 kg chump or barbecue
   lamb chops
2 tablespoons plain flour
¾ teaspoon salt

Trim any excess fat from the chops. Coat them with the seasoned flour, then fry on both sides in the hot butter or margarine. Lift out and place in a casserole.

1½ tablespoons butter or
   margarine
3 small onions peeled and cut
   into wedges
1 carrot scraped and diced
1 cup diced celery
½ cup diced green pepper
1 cup tomato purée
1 cup stock, or water and 1 soup
   cube
1 teaspoon vinegar
¼ teaspoon thyme
parsley to garnish

Add the onions, carrots, celery and green pepper to the pan and brown lightly. Place in the casserole.

Stir any remaining flour into the pan and stir until it browns, then add the tomato purée, stock, vinegar and thyme. Stir until boiling. Pour over the chops and vegetables in the casserole, cover and cook in a moderate oven (350° F, 180° C) for about 1½ hours or until the chops are tender. Serve with a parsley garnish.

Spiced Chops

5 forequarter chops
1 carrot scraped and sliced
1 medium onion peeled and
   sliced
1½ tablespoons plain flour
1 teaspoon sugar
½ teaspoon mustard
½ teaspoon curry powder
½ teaspoon mixed spice
½ teaspoon ground ginger
1 slightly rounded teaspoon salt
good pinch of pepper
2 tablespoons tomato sauce
2 tablespoons vinegar
1½ cups water

Trim any excess fat from the chops and place them in a lightly greased casserole. Cover with the sliced carrot and onion.

Mix the dry ingredients together in a small bowl and add the tomato sauce, vinegar and water. Pour over the meat in the casserole, cover and allow to stand for at least 1 hour to blend the flavours. Place in a moderate oven (350° F, 180° C) to cook for about 2 hours or until the chops are tender.

Spring Casserole

4 forequarter lamb chops
2 tablespoons seasoned plain
   flour
1 tablespoon butter

Trim any excess fat from the chops then coat them with the seasoned flour. Heat the butter in a pan and brown the chops on both sides. Lift out, drain on paper and place in a lightly

3 small onions
1 cup well-drained sweet corn
½ cup chopped celery
salt and pepper
½ cup tomato purée
½ cup stock, or water and 1
  soup cube
4 medium potatoes
1 tablespoon chopped parsley
  to garnish

greased casserole. Sprinkle with any remaining flour. Cover the chops with the sliced onions, corn and celery. Season well with salt and pepper.

Combine the tomato purée with the stock and pour into the casserole. Cover and cook in a moderate oven (350° F, 180° C) for 1 hour. Add the peeled and sliced potatoes, cover and return the casserole to the oven for a further 30 minutes. Serve sprinkled with the chopped parsley.

Sweet and Sour Casseroled Chops

1½ lb or 750 g shoulder or
  chump chops
1 tablespoon plain flour
1 teaspoon sugar
¼ teaspoon pepper
½ teaspoon salt
3 tablespoons tomato sauce
2 teaspoons Worcester sauce
1 tablespoon vinegar
1 cup water

Remove any excess fat and coat the chops in a mixture of flour, sugar, pepper and salt. Place in a greased casserole, sprinkling any remaining flour over the chops. Combine the tomato sauce and the Worcester sauce with the vinegar and water and pour over the chops. Cover and cook in a moderate oven (350° F, 180° C) for about 2 hours or until the chops are tender.

PASTA & EGGS

Beef Noodle Casserole

1 tablespoon butter
2 tablespoons minced onion
1 lb or 500 g finely minced steak
1 tablespoon plain flour
2 cups peeled and chopped
  tomatoes
1 tablespoon tomato sauce
1 bay-leaf
1 clove of garlic crushed
salt and pepper
$\frac{1}{2}$ lb or 250 g noodles
2 tablespoons grated Parmesan
  cheese
2 tablespoons soft white
  breadcrumbs

Melt the butter in a saucepan and add the onion, cook until golden, then add the meat and cook, stirring constantly until it changes colour. Now stir in the flour, the chopped tomatoes, tomato sauce, bay-leaf, garlic, and salt and pepper to taste. Cover and simmer for about 1 hour.

Cook the noodles in boiling salted water, then drain well. Put half of them in the bottom of a greased casserole and pour over the meat mixture. Sprinkle with the Parmesan cheese, cover with the remaining noodles, and finally with the breadcrumbs. Sprinkle with extra cheese if liked. Bake uncovered at 350° F (180° C) for about 30 minutes.

Cheese and Vegetable Casserole/Macaroni Vegetable Bake

Cheese and Vegetable Casserole

12 tiny white onions peeled
6 or 8 baby carrots scraped and
    cooked
1 cup green peas cooked
1 rounded tablespoon butter
2 level tablespoons plain flour
$1\frac{1}{4}$ cups milk
salt and pepper
1 chicken soup cube
2 eggs
1 tablespoon butter melted
2 tablespoons cream
1 cup grated cheese
bacon rolls and parsley to
    garnish

Place the onions in boiling salted water and cook until tender. Drain. Arrange the onions, carrots and peas in the bottom of a lightly greased shallow casserole.

Melt the butter in a saucepan, add the flour and stir until smooth, then cook for 1 or 2 minutes, but do not allow the mixture to brown. Add the milk and stir until the sauce boils and thickens. Flavour with salt and pepper to taste, and crumble in the soup cube. Simmer for 3 minutes. Pour this sauce over the vegetables in the casserole.

Beat the eggs with the tablespoon of melted butter and add the cream and the grated cheese, mixing well. Pour over the hot vegetable mixture and bake uncovered at 350° F (180° C) for about 25 minutes or until the top has set and is nicely browned. Top with some bacon rolls and garnish with parsley.

84

Cheese Custard Casserole

4 slices bread about $\frac{1}{4}$ inch thick,
    crusts removed
2 tablespoons butter
1 medium onion peeled and
    finely chopped
1 cup sliced mushrooms
1 cup diced cooked chicken,
    ham or tuna
2 cups shredded Cheddar cheese
2 teaspoons plain flour
4 eggs
2 teaspoons prepared mustard
1$\frac{1}{2}$ cups milk
$\frac{1}{2}$ teaspoon salt
$\frac{1}{2}$ teaspoon garlic salt
tomato wedges and parsley sprigs
    to garnish

Spread the bread slices with half the butter and arrange them buttered side down in a large casserole. Heat the remaining butter in a saucepan and sauté the onions and the mushrooms for about 5 minutes. Spoon evenly over the bread and cover with the chicken, ham or tuna.

Combine the cheese and flour and sprinkle over the ham. Beat together the eggs, mustard, milk, salt and garlic salt and pour over the ingredients in the casserole. Cover and refrigerate for at least 4 hours or overnight. Bake uncovered in a moderate oven (350° F, 180° C) for 25 to 30 minutes or until puffed and browned. Serve immediately, garnished with tomato wedges and parsley sprigs.

Curried Egg Casserole

6 hard-boiled eggs
$\frac{1}{3}$ cup mayonnaise
$\frac{1}{2}$ teaspoon salt
$\frac{1}{2}$ teaspoon paprika
$\frac{1}{4}$ teaspoon dry mustard
1 tablespoon melted butter
1 tablespoon plain flour
10$\frac{1}{2}$ oz or 298 g can cream of
    mushroom soup
1 soup can milk
$\frac{1}{2}$ cup shredded cheese
1 cup buttered breadcrumbs

Shell the eggs and cut them in half lengthwise. Remove the yolks and mash them, adding the mayonnaise, salt, paprika and dry mustard. Refill the egg whites with this mixture and place them in a shallow casserole which has been lightly greased.

Put the melted butter in a saucepan and add the flour. Stir until smooth, cook for 1 minute without browning, then add the soup and milk. Cook, stirring constantly, until the mixture boils and thickens. Add the cheese and stir until melted. Pour over the eggs in the casserole. Sprinkle the buttered crumbs round the edges of the casserole, making a border on the top. Bake uncovered in a moderate oven (350° F, 180° C) for 15 or 20 minutes or until the sauce bubbles and the crumbs brown.

Eggs Madras

3 tablespoons butter
3 teaspoons curry powder
1 cup chopped onion

Melt the butter in a saucepan and add the curry powder. Cook for 2 or 3 minutes, then add the onion and cook, stirring constantly, until tender

85

1½ tablespoons plain flour
1½ cups chicken broth
½ teaspoon salt
pinch of cayenne pepper
6 hard-boiled eggs sliced
1 teaspoon grated lemon rind
3 cups cooked rice
2 tablespoons cashew nuts
1 tablespoon sliced canned
  pimento
parsley to garnish

but not brown. Blend in the flour. Add the chicken broth, salt and pepper and cook for a few more minutes before folding in the eggs and lemon rind.

Add the cashew nuts and the sliced pimento to the cooked rice and place it in a lightly greased casserole. Top with the egg mixture, cover and reheat in a moderate oven (350° F, 180° C) for about 15 or 20 minutes. Serve with a parsley garnish.

Lasagne 1

1 lb or 500 g ground beef
1 tablespoon salad oil
1 clove of garlic crushed
1 tablespoon chopped parsley
½ teaspoon oregano
1 teaspoon salt
15 oz or 425 g can peeled
  tomatoes
5 oz or 142 g can tomato paste
pinch of pepper
½ lb or 250 g lasagne noodles
¾ lb or 375 g cream-style
  cottage cheese
½ lb or 250 g Mozzarella cheese
  thinly sliced
2 tablespoons grated Parmesan
  cheese

Brown the beef in the oil and add the garlic, parsley and oregano. Spoon off any excess fat and add the salt, tomatoes, tomato paste and pepper. Cover and simmer for 1 hour. Towards the end of the cooking period remove the lid and allow the liquid to reduce slightly.

Cook the noodles for 15 minutes in boiling water. Drain. In the bottom of a lightly greased casserole place one-third of the cooked noodles, then half the cottage cheese, half the Mozzarella and half the meat sauce. Add another third of the noodles then the remainder of the cottage cheese and Mozzarella, the remaining noodles and the rest of the meat sauce. Sprinkle with the Parmesan cheese. Bake uncovered in a moderate oven (350° F, 180° C) for 20 to 30 minutes or until heated through.

Lasagne 2

½ lb or 250 g lasagne or flat egg
  noodles
½ cup Parmesan cheese
½ cup grated Swiss or tasty
  Cheddar cheese
For the meat sauce
1 lb or 500 g finely minced steak
1 tablespoon oil
2 cloves of garlic crushed

Cook the noodles in plenty of boiling salted water until tender. Drain, run cold water through, then lift out and pat the surplus water off with a clean damp cloth.

To make the meat sauce, brown the minced steak in the hot oil. Add the remaining ingredients and bring to the boil, stirring lightly. Cover and simmer for ¾ to 1 hour. Season to taste with salt and pepper.

3 medium onions peeled and
 finely diced
2 rashers of bacon diced
1 carrot diced
3 bay-leaves
1 teaspoon oregano
salt and pepper
15 oz or 425 g can tomato soup
For the cream sauce
$1\frac{1}{2}$ tablespoons butter
3 tablespoons plain flour
1 cup unsweetened canned milk
1 beef soup cube
$\frac{1}{2}$ teaspoon salt
$\frac{1}{8}$ teaspoon nutmeg

To make the cream sauce, melt the butter in a saucepan and blend in the flour. Cook for 1 minute without browning, then add the milk. Cook, stirring constantly, until the sauce boils and thickens, then add the beef cube, salt and nutmeg.

Grease a large flat casserole, cover with a layer of meat sauce then a layer of the cooked lasagne with the ends turning up the sides of the dish. Cover with a layer of cream sauce and a sprinkling of each of the grated cheeses. Repeat layers, ending with cream sauce and cheese. Bake uncovered in a moderate oven (350° F, 180° C) for 25 or 30 minutes. Allow to stand for 5 minutes before serving.

Macaroni and Tuna Casserole

15 oz or 425 g can tuna
$\frac{1}{2}$ lb or 250 g macaroni
2 tablespoons butter
2 slightly rounded tablespoons
 plain flour
1 teaspoon dry mustard
$\frac{1}{2}$ teaspoon salt
pinch of pepper
$2\frac{1}{2}$ cups milk
2 tablespoons finely chopped
 parsley
2 tablespoons finely chopped
 onion
squeeze of lemon juice
2 oz or 60 g grated cheese
2 tomatoes peeled and sliced
salt, pepper and sugar
$\frac{1}{2}$ cup soft white breadcrumbs
 tossed in a little melted butter
lemon and parsley garnish

Drain and flake the tuna. Cook the macaroni in boiling salted water for 15 or 20 minutes or until tender, then drain and set aside.

Melt the butter in a saucepan, add the flour, mustard, salt and pepper and stir until smooth, then cook without browning for about 1 minute. Add the milk and stir until the sauce boils and thickens. Add the parsley, onion, lemon juice, drained and flaked tuna and the macaroni. Spoon into a lightly greased casserole and sprinkle with the cheese.

Arrange the tomato slices round the edge of the dish, seasoning them with salt, pepper and sugar. Top with the buttered breadcrumbs. Bake uncovered at 350° F (180° C) for about 30 minutes, then serve with a lemon and parsley garnish.

Macaroni Cheese de Luxe

4 oz or 125 g macaroni
1 tablespoon butter

Cook the macaroni in boiling salted water until tender. Drain well. Melt the butter in a saucepan,

1 rounded tablespoon plain flour
1 cup milk
1½ cups grated cheese
¼ teaspoon dry mustard
½ teaspoon salt
dash of pepper
1 cup fresh cream or cultured
    sour cream
1 cup diced cooked ham
chopped parsley to garnish

add the flour and stir until smooth, then cook without browning for 1 minute. Add the milk and cook, stirring constantly, until the sauce boils and thickens. Add the grated cheese, mustard, salt and pepper. Stir over medium heat until the cheese melts. Blend in the cream.

Place half the well-drained macaroni in the bottom of a greased casserole. Cover with half the ham and a spoonful of chopped parsley. Pour over half the cheese sauce, then top with the remaining ham, parsley and cheese sauce. Bake uncovered in a moderate oven (350° F, 180° C) for about 30 minutes. Serve garnished with parsley.

Macaroni Cheese Supreme

3½ cups cooked macaroni (about
    1¾ cups uncooked)
6¾ oz or 191 g can mushrooms
¼ cup chopped red or green
    pepper
¾ cup unsweetened canned milk
1¼ cups cubed processed cheese
1½ tablespoons chopped onion
2 teaspoons dry mustard
1 teaspoon salt
¼ teaspoon pepper
1 teaspoon Worcester sauce
4 thick slices of tomato
4 thin slices of cheese

Combine the cooked macaroni with the mushrooms and red pepper. In a saucepan combine the canned milk, processed cheese, onion, mustard, salt, pepper and Worcester sauce. Cook, stirring constantly, until the cheese melts. Add the macaroni mixture.

Turn the mixture into a lightly greased casserole and top with the tomato and cheese slices. Bake uncovered in a moderate oven (350° F, 180° C) for about 25 minutes or until the cheese melts and the macaroni mixture is thoroughly heated through.

Macaroni Cheese Supreme

Macaroni Meat Casserole

½ lb or 250 g macaroni
½ lb or 250 g minced steak
2 teaspoons butter (for meat)
½ cup chopped onion
1 teaspoon salt
good pinch of pepper
1½ tablespoons butter (for sauce)
1½ slightly rounded tablespoons
   plain flour
2 cups milk
½ teaspoon salt (for sauce)
pinch of paprika
½ teaspoon dry mustard
¾ cup grated cheese
¼ cup breadcrumbs
parsley to garnish

Cook the macaroni in boiling salted water for about 20 minutes or until tender. Drain well and set aside. Sauté the minced steak in 2 teaspoons butter until it changes colour. Add the onion and cook for a further 5 minutes. Season with the salt and pepper and set aside.

Melt 1½ tablespoons butter in a saucepan, blend in the flour and stir until smooth, then cook for 1 minute without browning. Add the milk and stir until the sauce boils and thickens. Add the salt, paprika and mustard and simmer for 3 minutes.

Place one-third of the macaroni in a lightly greased casserole, then add half the meat mixture and sprinkle with ⅔ of the grated cheese. Top with another one-third of the macaroni, the remaining meat and then the rest of the macaroni. Pour over the sauce and sprinkle with the remaining cheese and the breadcrumbs. Bake uncovered in a moderate oven (350° F, 180° C) for about 30 minutes or until the sauce bubbles and the cheese and breadcrumbs brown lightly.

Macaroni Vegetable Bake

1 cup cooked macaroni
1¼ cups grated cheese
2 small zucchini washed and
   thinly sliced
2 medium onions peeled and
   sliced
2 tomatoes peeled and cut into
   wedges
seasoned salt and pepper
pinch of oregano
2 oz or 60 g melted butter
3 hard-boiled eggs peeled and
   sliced
1 rounded tablespoon butter
1 rounded tablespoon plain flour
1½ cups milk
½ teaspoon salt

Combine the macaroni and ¼ cup of the grated cheese and place in the bottom of a lightly greased casserole. Add the prepared vegetables and season with the salt, pepper and oregano, then pour over the melted butter. Cover and cook in a moderate oven (350° F, 180° C) for about 25 minutes. Remove from the oven and placed the sliced eggs on top of the vegetables.

Melt the rounded tablespoon of butter in a saucepan, add the flour and stir until smooth, then cook for about 2 minutes but do not allow the mixture to brown. Add the milk and stir until the sauce boils and thickens, then season with the salt, mustard and cayenne pepper. Stir in the remaining cup of grated cheese and cook over medium heat until the cheese melts. Pour this mixture over the ingredients in the

¼ teaspoon dry mustard
pinch of cayenne pepper
paprika and parsley to garnish

casserole and if necessary return to the oven to reheat. Sprinkle with paprika and garnish with parsley before serving.

Macaroni with Sour Cream Topping

2 tablespoons butter
2 slightly rounded tablespoons
  plain flour
½ teaspoon salt
dash of cayenne pepper
¼ teaspoon mustard
1 teaspoon Worcester sauce
2½ cups milk
4 oz or 125 g macaroni cooked
  until tender
4 rounded tablespoons grated
  cheese
1 cup cultured sour cream or
  fresh cream
¼ cup finely chopped chives or
  shallots
½ cup crushed potato crisps
parsley and tomato to garnish

Melt the butter in a saucepan and add the flour, salt, cayenne and mustard. Stir until smooth, then cook for 1 minute without browning. Add the Worcester sauce and milk and cook, stirring constantly, until the sauce boils and thickens. Simmer for 2 minutes. Add the well-drained, cooked macaroni and 3 tablespoons of the grated cheese. Turn the mixture into a greased casserole. Pour over the sour cream and sprinkle with the chives or shallots, the crushed potato crisps and the remaining tablespoon of grated cheese. Bake uncovered at 300° F (150° C) for about 25 minutes or until the topping has browned and the sauce bubbles. Serve garnished with parsley and tomato slices.

Pasticcio

¼ lb or 125 g butter
2 medium onions peeled and
  finely chopped
1 lb or 500 g finely ground steak
salt and pepper
2 tablespoons tomato paste
1 clove garlic, crushed
1 tablespoon chopped parsley
¾ cup grated cheese
½ lb or 250 g lasagne noodles
For the cream sauce
2 tablespoons butter
3 level tablespoons plain flour
2 cups milk
3 tablespoons cream

Melt the butter in a saucepan, add the onions and cook until soft but not brown. Add the meat and cook, stirring constantly for about 3 minutes. Add salt and pepper to taste, then the tomato paste, garlic and parsley. Cover and simmer for 30 minutes, then blend in two-thirds (½ cup) of the grated cheese.

  Cook the lasagne in boiling salted water for 15 minutes. Drain. To make the cream sauce, melt the butter in a small saucepan, add the flour and stir until smooth, cook 2 minutes without browning, then add the milk and stir until the sauce boils and thickens. Add the cream, and season with salt and pepper. Line a lightly greased shallow casserole dish with half the

salt and pepper
1 egg

lasagne. Add the meat mixture, then top with the remainder of the lasagne. Beat the egg and stir into the cream sauce, then add the remaining $\frac{1}{4}$ cup of grated cheese. Pour over the lasagne in the casserole and bake uncovered in a moderate oven (350° F, 180° C) for about 40 minutes or until the top is lightly browned and the mixture heated through.

Stuffed Egg Casserole

6 hard-boiled eggs
$3\frac{1}{2}$ oz or 99 g can salmon
1 teaspoon butter
squeeze of lemon juice
salt and pepper
2 slightly rounded tablespoons
   butter (for sauce)
$\frac{1}{4}$ cup chopped green pepper
2 rounded tablespoons plain flour
$1\frac{3}{4}$ cups milk
1 teaspoon mustard
pinch of cayenne pepper
4 tablespoons grated cheese
tomato slices and green pepper
   rings (optional) to garnish

Cut the eggs in halves lengthwise and remove the yolks, keeping the white intact. Press the yolks through a sieve. Drain the salmon, reserving the liquid. Flake the flesh lightly, then combine it with the sieved egg yolk, butter, lemon juice, and salt and pepper to taste. Refill the egg-white cases with this mixture.

Melt the butter for the sauce in a saucepan, add the green pepper and sauté until soft. Add the flour, stir until smooth and cook for 2 minutes without browning. Add the milk and the liquid drained from the salmon, and season to taste with salt, the cayenne pepper and the mustard. Add half the grated cheese.

Place the eggs in a lightly greased casserole, pour over the cheese sauce, then sprinkle with the remainder of the grated cheese. Bake uncovered in a moderate oven (350° F, 180° C) for about 15 minutes or until the cheese melts and the sauce bubbles. Garnish with the tomato slices and a few green pepper rings if liked.

Supper Casserole

2 tablespoons butter
$1\frac{1}{2}$ slightly rounded tablespoons
   flour
$1\frac{1}{2}$ cups milk
salt and pepper
$\frac{1}{2}$ cup grated Cheddar cheese
6 hard-boiled eggs peeled and
   sliced

Melt $1\frac{1}{2}$ tablespoons of the butter in a saucepan and blend in the flour. Cook for 1 minute but do not allow it to brown. Add the milk and cook, stirring constantly until the sauce boils and thickens. Cook for 2 minutes, then season with salt and pepper. Add the cheese and stir until it has melted.

Place half the hard-boiled egg slices in a lightly

3 large tomatoes peeled and
  thickly sliced
3 cooked carrots cut into strips
$\frac{1}{4}$ cup buttered breadcrumbs

greased casserole, reserve 6 tomato slices for topping and arrange the remainder over the eggs. Spoon over some of the sauce, add the carrot strips, the remaining egg slices and then the rest of the sauce. Sprinkle the breadcrumbs over the top and arrange the reserved tomato slices. Dot with pieces of the remaining butter and bake uncovered at 375° F (190° C) for about 30 minutes.

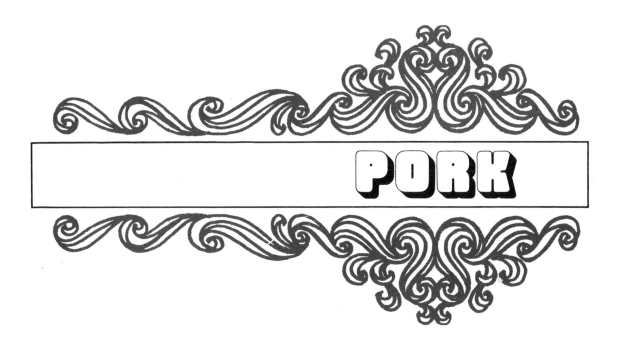

Creole Pork Chops

4 thick shoulder pork chops
seasoned plain flour
oil or fat for frying
10½ oz or 298 g can tomato soup
¼ soup can water
1 cup chopped celery
2 small onions peeled and
    chopped
1 green pepper seeded and
    chopped

Remove the surplus fat from the chops. Cover them lightly with seasoned flour and brown lightly on both sides in a little oil or fat. Drain on paper and place in a lightly greased casserole.

In a bowl combine the soup, water, celery, onion and green pepper. Mix well, then pour over the chops. Cover and cook in a moderate oven (350° F, 180° C) for about 1½ hours or until the chops are tender.

French Provincial Casserole

4 medium potatoes peeled and
    cut into ¼-inch-thick slices
¾ lb or 375 g pork fillet cut into
    1-inch cubes

Lightly grease a large casserole and place a layer of potatoes on the bottom. Top with half the pork and half the veal. Over the meat place the onion slices, half the parsley, 1 bay-leaf and 1 clove of

French Provincial Casserole

¾ lb or 375 g veal cut into
   1-inch cubes
2 medium onions peeled and
   sliced
⅓ cup finely chopped parsley
2 cloves of garlic crushed
2 bay-leaves
1½ teaspoons salt
¼ teaspoon pepper
1 cup white wine
½ cup stock, or water and 1
   rounded teaspoon of instant
   stock powder
1 tablespoon butter

garlic. Repeat with the remaining potatoes, pork, veal, onions, parsley and garlic, finishing with the other bay-leaf.

Sprinkle with salt and pepper, then slowly pour over the wine and stock. Place the butter on top. Cover and cook in a moderate oven (375° F, 180° C) for about 1½ hours or until the meats are tender.

Gourmet Pork Chops

6 thick pork chops
1 tablespoon plain flour
$\frac{1}{2}$ teaspoon salt
dash of pepper
$10\frac{1}{2}$ oz or 298 g can cream of
   mushroom soup
$\frac{3}{4}$ cup water
$\frac{1}{2}$ teaspoon ground ginger
$\frac{1}{4}$ teaspoon crushed rosemary
1 cup onion rings

Trim any excess fat from the chops and gently heat the trimmings in the pan until you have about 1 tablespoon of melted pork fat. Remove the trimmings. Coat the chops with a mixture of flour, salt and pepper, and brown them on both sides in the fat. Arrange in a single layer in a casserole.

Combine the soup, water, ginger and rosemary, pour over the chops and add half the onion rings. Cover and cook in a moderate oven (350° F, 180° C) for about 1 hour or until the pork is tender. Sprinkle with the remaining onion rings and replace in the oven without the lid to cook for a further 10 minutes. Serve with freshly boiled rice.

Italian Pork and Rice Casserole

1 medium onion peeled and sliced
1 clove of garlic peeled and
   crushed
1 tablespoon salad oil
$\frac{1}{2}$ cup stock
$10\frac{1}{2}$ oz or 298 g can tomato soup
1 soup can water
$7\frac{3}{4}$ oz or 220 g can buttered
   mushrooms
2 teaspoons chopped parsley
$1\frac{1}{2}$ lb or 750 g pork fillet
$\frac{1}{2}$ teaspoon salt
$\frac{1}{4}$ teaspoon pepper
2 teaspoons salad oil
1 cup uncooked rice
2 sliced onions
1 green pepper seeded and cut
   into slices
$\frac{1}{2}$ teaspoon salt

Place the onion, garlic and salad oil in a saucepan and sauté until the onion is tender. Add the stock, tomato soup, water, mushrooms and parsley. Stir until boiling, then simmer while you sauté the pork. Cut the pork into $\frac{1}{4}$-inch slices, sprinkle with the $\frac{1}{2}$ teaspoon salt and $\frac{1}{4}$ teaspoon pepper and sauté in the hot oil for about 10 minutes.

In a lightly greased casserole place half the sautéed pork, top with the rice which has been combined with half the tomato soup mixture, add the sliced onions, the rest of the pork, the green pepper, $\frac{1}{2}$ teaspoon salt and the remainder of the tomato soup mixture. Cover and cook in a moderate oven (350° F, 180° C) for $1\frac{1}{2}$ hours or until the rice is tender and most of the liquid has been absorbed.

Pineapple Pork Casserole

6 thick pork chops
For the stuffing
1 cup soft white breadcrumbs
$\frac{1}{2}$ teaspoon salt
dash of pepper
$\frac{1}{4}$ teaspoon marjoram
2 tablespoons minced celery
2 teaspoons minced onion or
    shallot
2 teaspoons butter, melted
1 teaspoon grated orange rind
$\frac{1}{2}$ cup well-drained crushed
    pineapple
For the sauce
$\frac{1}{2}$ cup diced onion
$\frac{1}{2}$ cup diced celery
2 tablespoons plain flour
salt and pepper
1 cup water
$\frac{1}{2}$ cup pineapple syrup drained
    from the can
1 beef soup cube crushed
2 teaspoons Worcester sauce

Trim any excess fat from the chops and cut a pocket in the meaty part of the chop. Combine all the ingredients for the stuffing in a bowl and mix well. Spoon some into the pocket of each chop and close the opening with a wooden cocktail pick.

Melt a little pork fat in a heavy-based pan and brown the chops on each side. Lift out and place in a casserole. Add the onion and celery to the drippings left in the pan and cook until the onion is lightly browned. Blend in the flour, with salt and pepper to taste, and cook for a few minutes, then add the water, pineapple syrup, soup cube and Worcester sauce. Stir until boiling, then pour over the chops in the casserole. Cover and cook in a moderate oven (350° F, 180° C) for 1 hour or until the chops are tender. Remove the cocktail picks and serve the chops with a parsley garnish.

Pork and Noodle Casserole

$\frac{1}{2}$ lb or 250 g noodles
1 lb or 500 g lean pork
2 onions chopped
3 cups chopped celery
15 oz or 425 g can tomatoes
2 teaspoons salt
$\frac{1}{4}$ teaspoon pepper
1 teaspoon thyme
$1\frac{1}{2}$ cups grated Cheddar cheese

Cook the noodles in boiling salted water until tender, then drain and set aside. Cut the pork into $\frac{1}{2}$-inch cubes and brown in a heavy-based pan, adding a little oil or any fat trimmed from the pork. Stir in the onion, celery, tomatoes, salt, pepper and thyme. Mix well, then heat until boiling. Simmer for 5 minutes, then stir in the noodles.

In a large, lightly greased casserole place one-third of the mixture, then one-third of the cheese. Continue in layers ending with cheese. Cover and cook in a moderate oven (350° F, 180° C) for 1 hour, then take the lid off and continue cooking for another 15 minutes to lightly brown the cheese.

Pork and Tomato Casserole

1½ lb or 750 g pork fillet
1 to 2 tablespoons plain flour
1 teaspoon salt
¼ teaspoon pepper
butter for frying
½ cup chopped onion
1 clove of garlic peeled and
    crushed
1 cup water
1 soup cube
2 or 3 tomatoes skinned and
    sliced
chopped parsley to garnish

Cut the fillet into thin slices. Mix together the flour, salt and pepper and use to dust the pieces of pork. Melt a little butter in a heavy-based pan and fry the pork quickly on both sides. Lift out, drain briefly and place in a lightly greased casserole.

Add the onion and garlic to the butter left in the pan (with a little more butter if necessary) and sauté until lightly browned. Lift out with a slotted spoon and place over the pork in the casserole.

Add the remaining flour to the pan and stir until golden, then add the water and soup cube and stir until the mixture boils and slightly thickens. Pour over the pork.

Dip the tomatoes in boiling water, drain, then peel off the skin. Cut into slices and place these in a layer over the ingredients in the casserole. Cover and cook in a moderate oven (350° F, 180° C) for about 30 minutes or until the pork is tender—the time will depend on how thinly you have sliced the pork fillet. Serve sprinkled with chopped parsley.

Pork and Vegetable Casserole

6 thick pork chops
1½ tablespoons plain flour
1 teaspoon salt
¼ teaspoon pepper
¼ cup dry sherry
¾ cup stock, or water and 1 soup
    cube
2 teaspoons chopped parsley
1 bay-leaf
6 small carrots scraped and cut
    into 2-inch pieces
1 onion peeled and sliced

Trim the fat from the chops, then gently heat the trimmings in a heavy-based pan until you have about 1½ tablespoons of liquid fat. Remove the trimmings.

Mix together the flour, salt and pepper and use to coat the chops. Brown the chops on both sides in the heated pork fat, lift out and drain on paper, then place in a lightly greased casserole.

Add any left-over flour to the pan and stir until brown, then stir in the sherry, stock or water. Keep stirring until boiling. Add the parsley and bay-leaf. Pour this gravy over the chops in the casserole and top with the carrots, and the onion which has been separated into rings. Cover and cook in a moderate oven (350° F, 180° C) for about 1½ hours or until the chops

97

are tender. Remove the bay-leaf and if necessary any excess fat.

Pork Chop Casserole

4 thick pork chops
seasoned plain flour
1 green pepper seeded and
　finely chopped
1 clove of garlic crushed
$\frac{1}{2}$ lb or 250 g mushrooms, sliced
1 tablespoon plain flour
1 teaspoon salt
$\frac{1}{4}$ teaspoon pepper
$\frac{1}{4}$ cup dry white wine
$\frac{1}{2}$ cup water
1 teaspoon mushroom-flavoured
　instant stock or soup cube
2 peeled and quartered tomatoes
parsley to garnish

Trim the chops of excess fat and heat the trimmings gently in a heavy-based pan till you have about 2 tablespoons liquid fat. Remove the trimmings. Coat the chops with seasoned flour and brown them on both sides. Lift out, drain on paper and place in a casserole.

Add the green pepper, garlic, and mushrooms to the pan and sauté them for about 5 minutes. Blend in the tablespoon of flour and the salt and pepper, cook until it browns lightly then add the wine, water and instant stock. Stir until boiling, then pour over the chops in the casserole. Add the tomatoes, then cover and cook in a moderate oven (350° F, 180° C) for about 45 minutes or until the chops are tender. Serve garnished with parsley.

Pork Chops with Orange Sauce

6 thick pork chops
1 teaspoon salt
good pinch of pepper
good pinch of paprika
1$\frac{1}{2}$ tablespoons plain flour
1 medium onion peeled and
　finely chopped
4 whole cloves
1$\frac{1}{2}$ cups stock, or water and 1
　soup cube
2 navel oranges
2 teaspoons brown sugar
1 tablespoon white wine
2 teaspoons cornflour
good pinch of cinnamon

Remove the surplus fat from the chops. Place the trimmings in a large heavy-based frying pan and cook until you have about 1$\frac{1}{2}$ tablespoons of liquid fat. Remove the trimmings.

Combine the salt, pepper, paprika and flour and use to coat the chops. Brown them in the liquid pork fat, then lift out, drain on paper and place in a lightly greased casserole.

Add the onion to the pan and cook until brown, then any flour left over from coating the chops. Brown this flour, add the cloves and half the stock and stir until boiling. Pour over the chops. Cover and cook in a moderate oven (350° F, 180° C) for about 1$\frac{1}{2}$ hours or until the chops are tender.

Meanwhile grate the rind from the oranges and set it aside. Working over a bowl, cut the rind, including the white membrane, from the oranges. Cut the flesh into sections and set aside. To the juice collected in the bowl add the grated rind, brown sugar, white wine and the remaining stock. Blend in the cornflour and cinnamon. Remove the casserole from the oven and stir in this orange-flavoured mixture. Arrange the orange sections on top, cover and cook for a further 10 or 15 minutes. Serve with freshly boiled rice.

Pork Fillet with Savoury Sauce

1 lb or 500 g pork fillet
2 tablespoons butter
1 medium onion peeled and
  chopped
1 tablespoon plain flour
1 teaspoon salt
dash of pepper
1 cup water
2 teaspoons instant mushroom
  stock
1 or 2 ripe tomatoes

Cut the pork into thin slices and dust them with a little of the flour. Heat 1 tablespoon of the butter in a heavy-based pan and fry the pork lightly on both sides. Lift out, drain on paper and place in a lightly greased casserole.

Add the onion to the dripping in the pan, cook until golden, then add the rest of the butter, the remainder of the flour left after dusting the pork, and the salt and the pepper. Cook, stirring constantly until the flour browns, then add the water and the instant stock and stir until the sauce boils and thickens. Pour over the pork in the casserole.

Skin and slice the tomatoes and place the slices on top of the meat and gravy in the casserole. Cover and cook in a moderate oven (350° F, 180° C) for about 35 or 40 minutes—the time will depend on how thinly you have sliced the pork.

Pork in Mushroom Sauce

$1\frac{1}{2}$ lb or 750 g boneless pork
1 tablespoon butter or lard
$\frac{1}{3}$ cup diced onion
1 tablespoon diced green pepper
$\frac{1}{4}$ lb or 250 g fresh mushrooms
  peeled and sliced
1 slightly rounded tablespoon
  plain flour
1 cup water or stock
1 soup cube
1 teaspoon salt
dash of pepper
dash of oregano
$\frac{1}{2}$ cup white wine

Trim the pork and cut it into cubes. Brown on all sides in the melted butter in a heavy-based pan. Lift out with a slotted spoon and place in a lightly greased casserole.

Add the onion and green pepper to the pan and sauté until both are tender. Lift out and add to the casserole. Sauté the mushrooms in the pan and add to the casserole. Sprinkle the flour into the pan and stir until brown, then add the water or stock, the crumbled soup cube and the salt, pepper and oregano. Stir until boiling, then add the wine. Pour over the ingredients in the casserole, cover and cook in a moderate oven (350° F, 180° C) for about $1\frac{1}{2}$ hours or until the pork is tender.

Pork Tenderloin and Mushrooms

2 large pork tenderloins
1 clove of garlic crushed
melted butter
salt and pepper
seasoned plain flour
3 tablespoons stock
½ lb or 250 g mushrooms sliced
2 tcaspoons butter
1 rounded teaspoon flour
3 tablespoons cream
For the apple stuffing
1 tablespoon butter
1 teaspoon chopped onion
¼ cup soft white breadcrumbs
½ cup finely chopped apple
¼ cup finely chopped celery
pinch of poultry seasoning

Cut the pork tenderloins almost through, then flatten them, using a meat mallet. Mix the garlic with melted butter and brush the surface of the pork lightly.

To make the apple stuffing melt the butter in a small saucepan, add the onion and sauté until soft but not brown. Add the breadcrumbs, apple, celery, poultry seasoning and some salt and pepper to taste. Spread this stuffing over the pork, then roll it up and secure with metal skewers or sew up with a coarse thread. Season the roll with salt and pepper and dredge with seasoned flour. Place in a shallow casserole, add the stock, cover and cook in a moderate oven (350° F, 180° C) for about 40 minutes.

Sauté the sliced mushrooms in the heated butter. Spread this over the pork and return the pork to the oven for about 10 minutes. Remove from the oven. Pour off the liquid and add it to the flour which has been blended with the cream, put in a saucepan, stir until boiling, then pour over the pork, cover and return the casserole to the oven for about 10 minutes.

Stuffed Pork and Vegetable Casserole

6 thick pork chops
1 small onion peeled and chopped
1 stalk of celery
1 tablespoon butter
¼ teaspoon mixed herbs
salt and pepper
1 cup soft white breadcrumbs
seasoned plain flour
fat from pork chops
1 tablespoon plain flour
1 cup water and 1 teaspoon
  instant stock
6 small carrots scraped and cut
  into 2-inch pieces
½ lb or 250 g green beans cut into
  chunky pieces

Remove the surplus fat from the chops and set it aside. Make a 1-inch slit in the fat side of each chop to form a pocket. Sauté the onion and celery in the butter, then add the pinch of herbs, salt and pepper to taste, the breadcrumbs, with a little milk if the mixture is too dry. Use this seasoning to stuff the chops, then coat them with seasoned flour.

In a heavy-based pan heat the fat which was removed from the chops until you have about 1 tablespoonful. Add the chops, brown them well on both sides, drain on paper and place in a lightly greased casserole. Season them with salt and pepper.

Add 1 tablespoon flour to the pan and cook, stirring well, until the mixture browns, then add the water and instant stock and keep stirring over medium heat until the gravy boils and thickens. Place the prepared vegetables around the chops in the casserole and pour over the gravy. Cover and cook in a moderate oven (350° F, 180° C) for about 1½ hours or until the chops are tender.

Sweet and Sour Pepper Pork

1 lb or 500 g pork fillets
1 medium green pepper
1 egg yolk
2 teaspoons water
2 teaspoons plain flour
2 teaspoons cornflour
salad oil
1 clove of garlic
For the seasoning sauce
2 teaspoons cornflour
¾ cup water
2 teaspoons chilli sauce
2 teaspoons soy sauce
1 tablespoon sugar
1½ tablespoons white wine vinegar
a few drops of hot pepper sauce or seasoned pepper

Cut the pork into 2-inch crosswise pieces then cut each of these into lengthwise strips about ¼ inch wide. Seed the green pepper and cut into ¼ inch strips. Prepare the seasoning sauce by blending the cornflour with the cold water then adding the remaining ingredients.

Beat the egg yolk with the 2 teaspoons of water, then blend in the flour and cornflour. Stir until smooth. Add the pork strips to this mixture and stir to coat each piece evenly. Heat some oil in a saucepan and add the pork pieces a few at a time. Cook, stirring occasionally, until the crust is a golden brown. This will take about 10 minutes. As you remove the pork from the pan drain it briefly on paper and place in a dish to keep hot.

Now heat 2 tablespoons of oil in the same pan and add the garlic. When it browns remove it and add the green pepper strips. Sauté for a few minutes, then add the seasoning sauce and cook, stirring constantly until the sauce boils and thickens. Add the pork and serve over freshly cooked rice.

Wine-braised Pork Chops

4 thick pork chops
seasoned plain flour
1 onion peeled and sliced
1 clove of garlic crushed
1 cup sliced mushrooms
1 tablespoon plain flour
1 teaspoon salt
¼ teaspoon pepper
½ cup white wine

Trim the excess fat from the chops and heat it gently in a heavy-based pan until you have about 2 tablespoons of liquid fat. Remove the trimmings.

Coat the chops with seasoned flour and fry them until brown on both sides in the pork fat. Lift out, drain on paper and place in a lightly greased casserole. Sauté the onion, garlic and mushrooms in the same pan, lift out and add to

½ cup water or stock
2 peeled and quartered tomatoes
1 small green pepper seeded and
   cut thinly into rings

the casserole. Blend the tablespoon of flour with the fat left in the pan, then cook until it is a golden colour. Season with the salt and pepper and add the white wine and water. Stir until boiling and add to the casserole. Place the tomatoes over the top, cover and cook in a moderate oven (350° F, 180° C) for about 1 hour or until the chops are tender. Garnish with the green pepper rings before serving.

RABBIT

Rabbit and Bacon Casserole

1 rabbit
2 tablespoons bacon fat or butter
1 medium onion peeled and
    finely chopped
1 slightly rounded tablespoon
    plain flour
2 cups stock, or water and 2
    teaspoons instant mushroom
    stock powder
1 bouquet garni
1 rounded teaspoon tomato purée
1 clove of garlic peeled and
    crushed
salt and pepper
4 rashers of bacon
2 tablespoons chopped shallots

Remove the kidneys from the rabbit and soak it in tepid water containing a little salt for about 1 hour. Drain, dry and cut into serving joints.

Heat the bacon fat in a pan (or in a casserole which will take hot-plate cooking) and brown each piece of rabbit. Drain on paper and place in a lightly greased casserole.

To the fat left in the pan add the onion and flour. Cook, stirring constantly, until it is a golden brown. Add the stock, bouquet garni, tomato purée and garlic and stir until boiling. Taste and add salt and pepper if necessary. Pour over the rabbit in the casserole, cover and cook in a moderate oven (350° F, 180° C) for about 1 hour. Now add the bacon, which has been cut into 1-inch pieces, and the chopped shallot. Return the casserole to the oven and cook for a further 30 to 45 minutes or until the rabbit is quite tender.

Rabbit and Bacon Scallop

2 rashers of bacon
1½ lb or 750 g rabbit fillets
4 cups shredded spinach
2 medium carrots scraped and
 cut into julienne strips
1 medium apple peeled, cored
 and thinly sliced
½ cup water
½ teaspoon Vegemite
½ cup cultured buttermilk
2 teaspoons chopped parsley to
 garnish

Remove the rind from the bacon, then stretch the bacon by running the flat blade of the knife along each rasher. Cut into pieces and wrap a piece round each rabbit fillet, securing with wooden cocktail picks. Place in a casserole. Layer the vegetables over the rabbit, ending with sliced apple. Pour the water over the contents of the casserole, cover and cook in a moderate oven (350° F, 180° C) for about 1 hour or until the rabbit is tender.

Strain off the liquid, add the Vegemite and buttermilk to it and return it to the casserole. Reheat, remove the cocktail picks, then serve sprinkled with chopped parsley.

Chicken can replace rabbit in this dish.

Rabbit Casserole

1½ lb or 750 g rabbit fillets
seasoned plain flour
3 rashers of bacon
1 medium onion peeled and
 chopped
1 cup sliced carrot
1 cup sliced parsnip
1½ tablespoons plain flour
2 cups chicken stock
salt and pepper

Coat the rabbit fillets with seasoned flour and set them aside. Cut the bacon rashers into 2-inch pieces and fry until the fat is clear. Remove from the pan. Add the rabbit pieces and fry until brown. Lift out, drain on paper and place in a casserole.

To the bacon fat left in the pan (you may need to add a little butter) add the onion, carrot and parsnip. Cook, stirring frequently, until the vegetables begin to brown. Lift out and add to the casserole. Stir in the 1½ tablespoons flour and cook until it browns. Add the chicken stock and keep stirring until the mixture boils and thickens slightly. Season with salt and pepper. Pour over the rabbit and vegetables in the casserole and top with the bacon pieces. Cover and cook in a moderate oven (350° F, 180° C) for 1½ to 2 hours or until the rabbit is tender.

Rabbit Casserole with Orange Dumplings

1½ lb or 750 g rabbit fillets
1½ tablespoons seasoned plain flour

Wash and dry the rabbit fillets and coat them with the seasoned flour. Heat the butter and oil in a

1 tablespoon butter
1 tablespoon oil
1 medium onion peeled and
    chopped
1 large parsnip scraped and diced
1 large carrot scraped and diced
1¼ cups stock, or water and
    1 soup cube
For the dumplings
1 cup self-raising flour
¼ teaspoon salt
1 teaspoon grated orange rind
2 teaspoons butter
orange juice and water to mix

pan and cook the rabbit pieces until brown. Lift out, drain and place in a lightly greased casserole.

Add the onion to the pan and stir over medium heat until brown. Lift out and add to the casserole. Sprinkle any flour remaining from coating the rabbit pieces into the pan, and stir until brown. Add the water or stock and stir until it boils and thickens. Add the carrot and parsnip and pour over the rabbit and onion in the casserole. Add a little salt and pepper, cover and cook in a moderate oven (350° F, 180° C) for about 1¼ hours.

To make the dumplings, sift the flour and salt into a bowl, add the grated orange rind and rub in the butter. Mix to a soft dough with the orange juice and water (you will need about 4½ tablespoons of liquid) and turn onto a floured board. Knead lightly and cut into 6. Knead each piece into a round and place on top of the rabbit in the casserole. Replace in the oven without the lid for about 15 minutes.

Rabbit Chasseur

1 young rabbit
2 teaspoons oil
1 tablespoon butter
1 tablespoon plain flour
⅓ cup chopped onion
⅓ cup white wine
1 cup stock
1 teaspoon tomato paste
1 bouquet garni
salt and pepper
1 cup sliced mushrooms
finely chopped parsley to garnish

Joint the rabbit and soak in cold water with a little salt for about 1 hour. Drain and dry. Heat the oil and butter in a pan, flour the rabbit joints and fry until golden on all sides. Lift out, drain on paper and place in a lightly greased casserole.

Add the onions to the pan and sauté until they begin to colour. Stir in any flour left over from coating the rabbit joints and stir until brown. Pour in the wine and stock and stir in the tomato paste, bouquet garni, salt and pepper. Stir until boiling, then pour over the rabbit in the casserole. Cover and cook in a moderate oven (350° F, 180° C) for about 1 hour or until the rabbit is tender. Half-way through the cooking time add the mushrooms. Before serving, sprinkle the top with finely chopped parsley.

Rabbit in Tomato Sauce

2 lb or 1 kg rabbit pieces
1 teaspoon salt
$\frac{1}{4}$ teaspoon pepper
1 tablespoon butter
1 large onion peeled and cut into
    eight pieces
$\frac{1}{2}$ cup chicken stock
$\frac{1}{2}$ cup white wine
$\frac{1}{2}$ teaspoon salt
pinch of pepper
1 cup tomato purée
1 teaspoon sugar
1 tablespoon plain flour
1 tablespoon water
$\frac{1}{2}$ cup chopped parsley to garnish

Sprinkle the rabbit pieces with the teaspoon of salt and the quarter teaspoon of pepper. Melt the butter in a heavy-based pan and brown the rabbit pieces well. Lift out and drain. Add the onion to the pan and cook until brown. Now add the chicken stock, wine, salt and pepper, and stir until boiling.

Place the rabbit pieces in a casserole and pour over the chicken stock mixture. Cover and cook in a moderate oven (350° F, 180° C) for about 45 minutes or until the rabbit is almost cooked.

Heat the tomato pureé in the pan in which the rabbit was browned, add the sugar and the flour which has been blended with the water and stir until boiling. Add to the casserole and cook for a further 15 minutes or until the rabbit is quite tender. Serve sprinkled with parsley.

SAUSAGES

Curried Tomato and Cheese Sausages

8 thick pork sausages
a little fat for frying
1 cup peeled and diced tomato
1 teaspoon curry powder
1 teaspoon sugar
2 rounded tablespoons grated
  cheese
salt and pepper
2 rashers of bacon cooked and
  crumbled
parsley to garnish

Place the sausages in a saucepan of cold water, bring slowly to the boil and simmer for 10 minutes. Drain well. Heat the fat in a frying pan and brown the sausages all over. Lift out and place in a lightly greased casserole.

Combine the tomato, curry powder, sugar, half the cheese and about $\frac{1}{2}$ teaspoon salt and a little pepper. Spoon this mixture over the sausages and top with the cooked and crumbled bacon. Sprinkle with the remainder of the cheese. Bake uncovered at 350° F (180° C) for about 20 minutes or until the cheese has melted and the sausages are cooked through. Serve with a parsley garnish.

Layered Sausage Casserole

6 thick sausages
1 tablespoon butter

Place the sausages in a saucepan of cold water and bring very slowly to the boil. Drain. Melt

2 onions peeled and thinly sliced
2 large potatoes peeled and
   sliced $\frac{1}{4}$ inch thick
salt and pepper
2 tablespoons finely chopped
   parsley
1 slightly rounded tablespoon
   plain flour
$1\frac{1}{4}$ cups water
1 beef soup cube
2 tablespoons tomato sauce
1 tablespoon Worcester sauce
tomato and parsley to garnish

the butter in a frying pan and brown the sausages on all sides. Lift out, drain on paper and cut each one in half lengthwise.

Arrange alternate layers of halved sausages, sliced onion and sliced potato in a lightly greased casserole, seasoning each layer with salt and pepper and sprinkling with some of the parsley.

Add the flour to the fat remaining in the pan and cook until brown. Add the water, the crushed soup cube, the tomato sauce and the Worcester sauce. Cook, stirring constantly until boiling, then pour over the contents of the casserole. Cover and cook in a moderate oven (350° F, 180° C) for 30 to 40 minutes. Serve garnished with tomato and parsley.

Sausage and Egg Casserole

4 hard-boiled eggs
2 tablespoons butter
$\frac{1}{4}$ cup plain flour
$\frac{1}{2}$ teaspoon salt
dash of pepper
2 cups milk
15 oz or 425 g can kernel-style
   corn well drained
2 tablespoons chopped parsley
1 lb or 500 g pork sausage-mince
   browned and drained of any
   fat
1 cup buttered breadcrumbs
parsley to garnish

Slice two of the eggs into the base of a lightly greased large (3-pint) casserole. Melt the butter in a saucepan, blend in the flour, salt and pepper. Cook for 1 minute without browning, then add the milk and cook, stirring constantly, until the sauce boils and thickens. Stir in the well-drained corn and chopped parsley and cook for 2 or 3 minutes.

Pour half the sauce over the eggs in the casserole, then arrange the pork mince in a layer on top. Pour over the rest of the sauce and arrange the remaining two sliced eggs on top. Sprinkle with the buttered breadcrumbs and bake uncovered in a moderate oven (350° F, 180° C) for 20 to 25 minutes or until the crumbs are brown and the casserole heated through. Serve garnished with parsley.

Sausage and Tomato Casserole

$1\frac{1}{2}$ lb or 750 g pork or beef
   sausage-mince
1 tablespoon chopped parsley
2 tablespoons chopped onion
2 tablespoons scraped and
   chopped or sliced carrot

Combine the sausage-mince with the parsley, onion, carrot, celery, lemon rind, salt and pepper. Mix thoroughly. Grease a shallow casserole and spread one-third of the meat mixture on the bottom, cover with half the sliced tomatoes, top with another one-third of the meat mixture and

2 tablespoons finely chopped
  celery
1 teaspoon grated lemon rind
1 teaspoon salt
dash of pepper
2 large tomatoes peeled and
  sliced
2 rounded tablespoons soft white
  breadcrumbs
1 tablespoon milk
1 tablespoon tomato sauce
  (optional)

the remaining tomato slices. Finally cover with the remaining meat mixture.

Combine the milk with the breadcrumbs and sprinkle over the top, then drizzle over the tomato sauce (if used). Put the lid on and bake in a moderate oven (350° F, 180° C) for about 30 minutes. Drain away any surplus fat before serving.

Sausage Casserole

12 thick pork sausages
6 rashers of bacon
2 small carrots scraped and sliced
2 medium onions peeled and
  sliced
$10\frac{1}{2}$ oz or 298 g can tomato soup
1 tablespoon sugar

Separate the sausages, cut the bacon rashers in half and wrap a piece of bacon round each sausage, securing it with a wooden cocktail pick. Brown lightly in a frying pan, then remove the cocktail picks.

Arrange the sausages in a lightly greased casserole and add the carrot and onion slices. Mix the soup and sugar in a saucepan and heat to dissolve the sugar. Pour over the ingredients in the casserole. Cover and cook in a moderate oven (350° F, 180° C) for about $1\frac{1}{4}$ hours.

Merial

Sausages in Barbecue Sauce

8 pork or beef sausages
2 tablespoons fat
1 medium onion peeled and
  sliced
2 tablespoons plain flour
3 tablespoons vinegar
1 tablespoon brown sugar
1 tablespoon sweet chutney
$\frac{3}{4}$ cup diced celery
1 tablespoon Worcester sauce
$\frac{1}{2}$ teaspoon mixed mustard
$1\frac{1}{4}$ cups water
salt and pepper
chopped parsley to garnish

Brown the sausages in the hot fat, then remove from the pan. Sauté the onion slices till brown, leave them in the pan, and add the flour. Stir until smooth, then cook, stirring constantly, until the mixture browns. Stir in the vinegar, brown sugar, chutney, celery, Worcester sauce, mustard and water. Now add the browned sausages and season to taste with salt and pepper.

Transfer to a casserole, cover and cook in a moderate oven (350° F, 180° C) for about 30 minutes. Serve sprinkled with chopped parsley and accompany with fried pineapple rings.

Sausages Mandalay/Curried Tomato and Cheese Sausages

Sausages Mandalay

8 thick pork sausages
fat for frying
2 tablespoons diced onion
2 teaspoons curry powder
1 small apple peeled and diced
1 tablespoon plain flour
1 cup beef stock
1 teaspoon lemon juice
salt and pepper

Place the sausages in a saucepan with cold water, bring to the boil and simmer for 10 minutes. Drain well. Place them in a frying pan with a little hot fat and cook until well browned on all sides, then lift them from the pan and drain away all but about 2 tablespoons of fat. Add the onion and the curry powder to the pan, blend until smooth, then cook for 5 minutes. Stir in the apple and flour, blend well, and cook for a further 3 minutes.

Add the stock, lemon juice, salt and pepper and stir until the mixture boils and thickens. Place the sausages in a lightly greased casserole and pour over the curry sauce. Cover and cook in a moderate oven (350° F, 180° C) for about 20 minutes. Serve with mashed potato or freshly boiled rice.

Savoury Sausages

1½ to 2 lb or 750 g to 1 kg thick beef or pork sausages
a little fat
1 large onion peeled and sliced
1 clove of garlic crushed
3 tomatoes peeled and sliced
2 slightly rounded tablespoons plain flour
1 teaspoon salt
dash of pepper
½ teaspoon dry mustard
1 tablespoon tomato sauce
1 teaspoon Worcester sauce
2 teaspoons lemon juice
1 teaspoon brown sugar
1½ cups beef stock

Place the sausages in a bowl and cover with boiling water. Allow to stand for about 5 minutes, then drain well. Prick each sausage several times with a fork. Heat a little fat in a pan and brown the sausages on all sides. Drain on paper and place in a casserole.

In the fat remaining in the pan fry the sliced onion until brown, then add the garlic and tomatoes and continue to cook for a few minutes. Sprinkle over the flour, salt, pepper and mustard. Blend well, then cook for a few minutes. Add the tomato sauce, Worcester sauce, lemon juice, brown sugar and stock. Stir until the mixture boils and thickens. Pour over the sausages in the casserole, cover and cook in a moderate oven (350° F, 180° C) for about 30 minutes.

Scalloped Corn and Sausage

1 teaspoon oil
1 lb or 500 g pork sausage-mince
1½ tablespoons plain flour
1¼ cups milk
1 teaspoon salt
dash of pepper
2 teaspoons chopped parsley
15 oz or 425 g can kernel-style corn well drained
1 tomato peeled and sliced

Heat the oil in a pan, take spoonfuls of the sausage-mince, drop each into the heated oil in the pan and cook until brown. Lift out.

Pour away all but 1 tablespoon of oil, add the flour to the pan and stir until well blended. Add the milk. Cook, stirring constantly, until the mixture boils and thickens. Add the salt, pepper, parsley and drained corn.

Pour the corn mixture into a shallow greased casserole and add the pork. Top with the tomato slices. Cover and cook in a moderate oven (350° F, 180° C) for about 20 minutes.

Swiss Sausages

2 lb or 1 kg thick sausages
¼ cup plain flour

Put the sausages into a saucepan, cover with cold water and bring slowly to just below boiling

1½ teaspoons salt
good pinch of pepper
1 teaspoon dry mustard
½ teaspoon brown sugar
3 tablespoons butter or margarine
1 medium onion peeled and
  finely chopped
1 cup water
2 teaspoons Worcester sauce
2 teaspoons tomato sauce
1 bay-leaf

point. Drain well. Combine the flour, salt, pepper, mustard and sugar and use to coat the sausages.

Heat the butter in a pan and brown the coated sausages all over. Lift out and set aside.

Add the onion to the fat left in the pan and cook until it is golden. Add the flour remaining from coating the sausages, and stir until brown. Add the water, Worcester sauce, tomato sauce and bay-leaf. Place the browned sausages in a lightly greased casserole and pour over the gravy. Cover and cook in a moderate oven (350° F, 180° C) for about 45 minutes. Remove the bay-leaf before serving.

American Veal with Bananas

4 firm but ripe bananas
soft white breadcrumbs
mixed herbs
butter for frying
8 veal cutlets
seasoned plain flour
1 rounded tablespoon plain flour
$1\frac{1}{4}$ cups stock
1 tablespoon chopped onion
1 tablespoon chopped green
   pepper
$\frac{1}{2}$ cup dry sherry
bacon rolls and parsley sprigs to
   garnish

Peel the bananas and cut each one in half cross-wise. Roll in breadcrumbs into which has been blended a small quantity of mixed herbs to taste. Brown lightly in melted butter.

Trim the veal, beating if too thick. Roll each piece round a banana half, securing with wooden cocktail picks. Coat with seasoned flour and brown lightly in melted butter in the pan in which the bananas were browned. Remove and place in a casserole.

Blend the tablespoon of flour with the butter in the pan (add extra butter if necessary). Stir in the stock, onion, green pepper and sherry and keep stirring until boiling. Pour over the rolls in the casserole. Cover and cook in a moderate oven (350° F, 180° C) for about 1 hour or until the veal is tender. Remove the cocktail

*American Veal
with Bananas*

picks and serve garnished with grilled or baked bacon rolls and sprigs of parsley.

Barbecued Veal with Rice

1½ lb or 750 g veal steak cut into
   1-inch cubes
2 tablespoons butter
1 slightly rounded tablespoon
   plain flour
½ teaspoon salt
dash of pepper
½ cup tomato purée
½ cup water
1 teaspoon Worcester sauce
½ teaspoon brown sugar
1 teaspoon prepared mustard
¼ cup diced onion
¼ cup diced celery

Melt the butter in a pan and brown the veal slowly on all sides. Lift out and place in a casserole. Add the flour to the pan drippings and cook, stirring until lightly browned, then add the salt and pepper, tomato purée and water. Stir until boiling, then season with the Worcester sauce, brown sugar, prepared mustard, onion and celery. Pour over the veal in the casserole, cover and cook in a moderate oven (350° F, 180° C) for about 2 hours.

Mound freshly cooked rice round the edge of the serving dish and fill the centre with the meat. Or serve directly from the casserole, spooning the veal mixture over the rice.

Braised Veal with Prosciutto and Cheese

2 lb or 1 kg veal steak
8 thin slices, about 3 inches
    square, Gruyère cheese
8 thin slices prosciutto (Italian
    style ham)
salt
freshly ground black pepper
plain flour
3 tablespoons butter
1 wine-glass white wine
$\frac{3}{4}$ cup chicken stock

Cut the veal into 4-inch squares and pound each piece with a meat mallet until thin. On each piece of veal place a square of cheese and top this with one of prosciutto. Fold the veal over the filling and secure with wooden cocktail picks. Season each with salt and pepper and dust with flour.

Place the butter in a large heavy-based pan and brown the veal a few rolls at a time. As they are browned place them in a lightly greased casserole.

Add an extra tablespoon of flour to the pan and stir until brown, scraping any brown bits from the bottom of the pan. Add the wine and stock and stir until boiling.

Pour the liquid over the veal in the casserole, cover and cook in a moderate oven (350° F, 180° C) for about 30 minutes or until the veal is tender. Taste the gravy and add a little more salt and pepper if required. Remove the cocktail picks before serving.

Curried Veal New Mexico Style

1 lb or 500 g minced veal
$1\frac{1}{2}$ cups soft white breadcrumbs
$\frac{1}{2}$ cup stock
1 egg
salt and pepper
$\frac{1}{4}$ cup finely chopped onion
2 tablespoons minced parsley
1 tablespoon minced celery
1 tablespoon minced chives
seasoned plain flour
3 tablespoons bacon drippings
    or butter
2 tablespoons finely chopped
    onion (for gravy)
$1\frac{1}{2}$ tablespoons plain flour
2 teaspoons curry powder
1 cup hot water
1 onion soup cube
parsley sprigs to garnish

Combine the veal, breadcrumbs, stock, beaten egg, salt and pepper to taste, $\frac{1}{4}$ cup onion, and the parsley, celery and chives. Mix lightly but thoroughly and form into 12 even-sized balls, using seasoned flour.

Heat the bacon drippings in a heavy-based pan and brown the veal balls on all sides. Remove from the pan and place in a casserole.

Add the 2 tablespoons onion, the flour and the curry powder to the drippings left in the pan, stir until smooth, then cook for 2 minutes. Add the water and the crumbled soup cube and stir until boiling. Pour over the meatballs in the casserole. Cover and cook in a moderate oven (350° F, 180° C) for about 45 minutes. Serve over freshly boiled rice with parsley sprigs to garnish.

Hawaiian Veal Curry

2 tablespoons butter
1 medium onion peeled and
  chopped
2 cloves of garlic peeled and
  crushed
3 lb or 1.5 kg lean veal cut into
  1-inch cubes
2 tablespoons seasoned plain
  flour
$10\frac{1}{2}$ oz or 298 g can cream of
  mushroom soup
$\frac{1}{2}$ soup can milk
$\frac{1}{4}$ teaspoon pepper
squeeze of lemon juice
1 to $1\frac{1}{2}$ tablespoons curry powder
15 oz or 425 g can pineapple
  pieces

Place the butter in a pan and sauté the onion until tender. Add the garlic. Toss the veal cubes in the seasoned flour, add to the onion and garlic butter mixture in the pan and cook until the veal changes colour. Now add the soup, milk, pepper, lemon juice, and curry powder. Stir until boiling. Pour into a lightly greased casserole, cover and cook in a moderate oven (350° F, 180° C) for about 1 hour or until the veal is almost tender.

Drain the pineapple pieces from the juice and add them to the casserole. Stir very lightly to mix the pineapple with the veal, then replace the lid and cook for a further 15 minutes or until the veal is tender. Serve with freshly boiled rice and your favourite curry accompaniments.

Hawaiian Veal Curry

Hungarian Veal Birds

8 veal cutlets
salt and pepper
paprika
pinch of thyme
2 cups soft white breadcrumbs
1 tablespoon chopped parsley
1 tablespoon minced onion
1 tablespoon minced shallot
1 tablespoon chopped mushrooms
1 tablespoon minced gherkins
1 tablespoon chopped stuffed
  olives
$\frac{1}{4}$ cup butter melted
seasoned plain flour
3 tablespoons butter (for frying)
$1\frac{1}{2}$ tablespoons plain flour
1 cup stock
1 clove of garlic crushed

Pound the cutlets with a meat mallet until they are very thin. Season them with salt, pepper, paprika and thyme and set aside while you prepare the stuffing.

Combine the breadcrumbs, chopped parsley, onion, shallot, mushroom, gherkin, olive and melted butter. Season with salt and pepper. Divide the stuffing evenly among the veal cutlets, roll each one up and secure with fine twine or with wooden cocktail picks. Coat with seasoned flour.

Heat the butter in a heavy-based frying pan and brown the veal birds on all sides. Remove from the pan and place in a lightly greased casserole.

To the drippings in the pan (add a little more butter if needed) add the flour, stir until smooth, then cook until brown. Add the stock, the crushed garlic and some salt and pepper, and stir until the mixture boils and slightly thickens. Pour over the veal birds, cover and cook in a moderate oven (350° F, 180° C) for about 1 hour or until the meat is tender. Remove the twine or the cocktail picks before serving.

Hungarian Veal Paprika

2 lb or 1 kg boneless veal cut
  into 1-inch cubes
3 tablespoons plain flour
1 teaspoon salt
dash of pepper
1 teaspoon mustard
3 tablespoons melted butter
2 medium onions peeled and
  chopped
1 clove of garlic peeled and
  crushed
1 cup stock, or water and 1 soup
  cube
1 cup tomato purée

Toss the veal cubes in a mixture consisting of 2 tablespoons of the flour, the salt, pepper and mustard. Heat the butter in a pan and fry the chopped onions until soft, mix in the garlic, then remove both with a slotted spoon. Add the veal to the pan and fry until it is lightly coloured.

Place the onion, garlic and veal in a lightly greased casserole. Use a little more butter in the pan if necessary, and add any flour left over from coating the veal plus the remaining table-spoonful. Cook, stirring constantly, until it browns. Add the stock, tomato purée and lemon juice and stir until boiling. Pour over the veal in the casserole. Add the paprika and mushrooms,

squeeze of lemon juice
1 tablespoon paprika
$\frac{1}{2}$ cup button mushrooms
$\frac{1}{4}$ to $\frac{1}{2}$ cup cultured sour cream
chopped parsley to garnish

cover and cook in a moderate oven (350° F, 180° C) for about 1$\frac{1}{2}$ hours or until the veal is tender. Just before serving, pour the sour cream on top and sprinkle with chopped parsley.

Red Scaloppini

6 veal cutlets thinly sliced
$\frac{1}{2}$ cup plain flour
1 teaspoon salt
pinch of pepper
3 tablespoons butter
1 tablespoon oil
1 onion peeled and sliced
$\frac{1}{2}$ lb or 250 g cultivated
   mushrooms sliced
2 cloves of garlic crushed
1 tablespoon white vinegar
1 tablespoon soy sauce
2 tablespoons tomato paste
$\frac{1}{3}$ cup sherry
1 cup chicken stock
1$\frac{1}{2}$ teaspoons oregano
1 cup grated cheese
2 tablespoons grated Parmesan
   cheese (optional)
parsley sprigs to garnish

Pound the veal until very thin and coat well with a mixture of flour, salt and pepper. Heat half the butter and the oil in a heavy-based pan and brown the meat quickly on all sides. Lift out and place in a lightly greased casserole.

Add the remaining butter to the pan and sauté the sliced onion and mushrooms and the garlic for 5 minutes. Add the vinegar, soy sauce, tomato paste, sherry, stock and oregano.

Stir until boiling, pour over the meat in the casserole, cover and cook in a moderate oven (350° F, 180° C) for about 1 hour or until the veal is tender. Remove from the oven and add the cheese, stirring until just melted. Serve garnished with parsley sprigs and, if liked, with freshly boiled rice.

Sweet and Sour Veal

15 oz or 425 g can pineapple
   pieces
1$\frac{1}{2}$ lb or 750 g veal cut into cubes
1 tablespoon butter
1 cup chopped celery
$\frac{1}{2}$ cup chopped onion
1 teaspoon salt
dash of pepper
1 chicken soup cube dissolved
   in $\frac{1}{2}$ cup hot water
$\frac{1}{2}$ lb or 250 g bean sprouts

Drain the pineapple, reserving the juice. Brown the veal in hot butter, then add the celery, onion, salt, pepper, the stock made from the soup cube, and the syrup drained from the pineapple. Stir until boiling, then transfer to a casserole, cover and cook in a moderate oven (350° F, 180° C) for about 1$\frac{1}{2}$ hours. When the veal is tender, add the pineapple and the bean sprouts.

Blend the cornflour with the vinegar, soy sauce and monosodium glutamate. Remove the casserole from the oven, stir in the blended

2 scant tablespoons cornflour
$\frac{1}{4}$ cup vinegar
$1\frac{1}{2}$ tablespoons soy sauce
$\frac{1}{2}$ teaspoon monosodium
    glutamate

mixture, then cover and return it to the oven for a further 15 minutes. Serve with freshly boiled rice.

Veal Almondine

2 lb or 1 kg thin veal cutlets
3 tablespoons butter (for frying)
$15\frac{1}{2}$ oz or 439 g can condensed
    chicken soup
parsley to garnish
For the stuffing
1 tablespoon butter
1 medium onion peeled and
    finely chopped
$\frac{1}{2}$ lb or 250 g chicken livers
2 cloves of garlic crushed or
    minced
1 tablespoon finely chopped
    parsley
$\frac{1}{2}$ cup soft white breadcrumbs
1 teaspoon salt
pinch of pepper
For the gravy
1 medium onion finely minced
1 clove of garlic crushed or
    minced
$\frac{1}{4}$ cup plain flour
1 cup cultured sour cream
$1\frac{1}{2}$ to 2 tablespoons slivered
    almonds
paprika

Flatten the veal with a meat mallet or rolling-pin: each piece should be about 3 inches by 4 or 5 inches. Set aside. Heat the butter for the stuffing and fry the onion in it until soft but not brown. Add the chopped chicken livers and garlic and heat until they are just cooked. Remove from the pan and, if necessary, chop the livers a little finer. Combine the liver mixture with the parsley, breadcrumbs, salt and pepper. Mix well. Spread some of the stuffing on each piece of veal to within $\frac{1}{2}$ inch of the edges. Roll up tightly and secure each roll with wooden cocktail picks.

Heat the 3 tablespoons of butter in a heavy-based pan and cook the veal rolls until brown on all sides. Remove and drain well. Arrange the rolls in a single layer in a lightly greased casserole. Pour over the undiluted chicken soup. Cover and cook in a moderate oven (350° F, 180° C) for about 45 minutes or until the rolls are tender. Remove the rolls, drain lightly and remove the cocktail picks.

Drain the liquid from the casserole into the pan used to fry the rolls. Bring to the boil, scraping any browned pieces from the bottom or sides of the pan. Strain and set aside. Now make the gravy by heating the reserved butter (or about 1 tablespoon), add the onion and cook until brown, then stir in the garlic. Add the flour and stir until smooth and brown. Stir in the chicken soup mixture that was set aside, and stir until it boils and thickens. Add the cream and reheat. Arrange the veal rolls in a casserole, pour over the gravy and sprinkle with the slivered almonds and paprika. Serve garnished with parsley.

Veal Almondine

Veal Casserole with Potato Soufflé

$\frac{1}{2}$ lb or 250 g chicken livers
    chopped
1 tablespoon butter or oil
1 medium onion peeled and
    chopped
2 lb or 1 kg veal steak sliced
    thinly
2 tablespoons plain flour
$\frac{3}{4}$ cup chicken stock, or water
    and 1 soup cube
$\frac{3}{4}$ cup white wine
1 teaspoon salt
8 whole baby carrots scraped
$\frac{1}{2}$ packet instant mashed potato

Using a large pan quickly brown the chicken livers in the butter. Remove with a slotted spoon and set aside. Fry the onion in the pan until golden. Toss the veal slices in the flour, then fry quickly in the same pan, adding more butter as required. Lift out, add the remainder of the flour to the pan and stir over medium heat until brown. Add the stock and wine and stir until boiling. Return the meat to the pan, season with the salt and add the carrots. Transfer to a lightly greased casserole. Cover and cook in a moderate oven (350° F, 180° C) for about 40 minutes or until almost tender.

Prepare the instant mashed potato according

¼ cup grated Parmesan cheese
2 eggs separated

to the instructions on the packet. Mix in the cheese, then add the egg yolks one at a time. Beat the egg whites until stiff and fold into the potato mixture.

Add the chicken livers to the casserole, then spread the potato soufflé on top. Bake uncovered for 30 minutes or until the potato is puffed and lightly browned.

Veal Casserole with Spring Vegetables

1 large onion peeled and finely
  chopped
1 carrot scraped and chopped
1 tablespoon butter
2½ lb or 1.5 kg veal cubed
1½ cups water
½ teaspoon thyme
1 bay-leaf
1 teaspoon salt
½ cup cream
1 dessertspoon cornflour
2 egg yolks
15½ oz or 439 g can asparagus
1 cup freshly cooked peas

Cook the chopped onion and carrot in the butter in a large heavy-based pan until soft but not brown, stirring occasionally. Add the veal, cover and cook, stirring occasionally until the meat changes colour and releases the juices. Turn the mixture into a lightly greased casserole. Add the water, thyme, bay-leaf and salt, cover and cook in a moderate oven (350° F, 180° C) for about 2 hours or until the meat is tender.

Lift the meat and vegetables out with a slotted spoon and drain the liquid into a small saucepan. Return the meat, onion and carrot to the casserole and keep hot.

Blend the cream and cornflour until smooth and stir into the hot liquid in the saucepan. Cook, stirring constantly, until the mixture boils and thickens. Take a little of this liquid and mix with the lightly beaten egg yolks, stir this into the liquid in the saucepan and cook for 1 minute. Pour over the meat and vegetables in the casserole.

Arrange the drained asparagus and cooked peas on top, cover and cook for a further 10 minutes or until heated through.

Veal Cutlet Casserole

2½ tablespoons plain flour
½ teaspoon salt
6 veal cutlets
2 tablespoons fat
1¼ cups stock, or water and 1
  soup cube

Mix 1½ tablespoons of the flour with the salt and rub over the veal cutlets. Melt the fat in a heavy-based pan and brown the cutlets on both sides. Lift out and place in a casserole.

Add the remaining tablespoon of flour to the drippings in the pan, stir until smooth and

½ teaspoon mustard
grated rind of ½ lemon
1 tablespoon soy sauce
1 teaspoon brown sugar
½ teaspoon paprika
salt and pepper
2 tablespoons sherry (optional)
1 large onion peeled and chopped
1 clove of garlic crushed
tomato wedges and parsley sprigs
   to garnish

brown, add the stock or water and stir until the mixture boils and thickens. Now add the mustard, lemon rind, soy sauce, brown sugar, paprika, salt and pepper to taste, and the sherry if used. Sprinkle the chopped onion and the crushed garlic over the cutlets in the casserole and pour over the gravy. Cover and cook in a moderate oven (350° F, 180° C) for 1½ to 2 hours, or until the veal is tender. Serve garnished with tomato wedges and parsley sprigs.

Veal Cutlets with Pineapple

6 veal cutlets
2 tablespoons plain flour
1 teaspoon salt
dash of pepper
2 tablespoons butter
½ cup pineapple syrup
2 tablespoons lemon juice
1 tablespoon Worcester sauce
6 well-drained pineapple slices
butter for frying
parsley sprigs to garnish

Trim the veal and flatten with a meat mallet, then coat with the flour, salt and pepper. Heat the butter in a pan and brown the veal on both sides. Drain on paper and place in a lightly greased casserole.

Blend 1 tablespoon of the remaining flour in the drippings in the pan and stir until lightly browned. Add the pineapple syrup, lemon juice, and Worcester sauce and stir until boiling. Pour this gravy over the veal in the casserole, cover and cook in a moderate oven (350° F, 180° C) for about 1 hour or until tender. When ready to serve, top the casserole with the pineapple slices which have been browned in a little butter in a pan or in a shallow dish in the oven. Serve with a parsley garnish.

Veal Mozzarella

6 veal cutlets
2 tablespoons plain flour
1 egg
2 tablespoons milk
1 teaspoon salt
1 cup soft white breadcrumbs
¼ cup cooking oil
1 small onion peeled and chopped
¼ cup chopped green pepper

Coat the cutlets lightly with flour. Combine the slightly beaten egg with the milk and salt. Dip the cutlets in this mixture, then cover with the breadcrumbs. Heat the oil in a large heavy-based pan and brown the meat on both sides. Drain on paper and place in a casserole.

Add an extra tablespoon of oil to the pan and sauté the chopped onion and green pepper for about 5 minutes. Stir in the tomato purée, wine,

1 cup tomato purée
¼ cup white wine
1 teaspoon garlic salt
pinch of pepper
pinch of marjoram
pinch of oregano
4 oz or 125 g Mozzarella cheese

garlic salt, pepper, marjoram and oregano. Stir until boiling, simmer for 10 minutes, then pour over the cutlets in the casserole. Cover and cook in a moderate oven (350° F, 180° C) for 35 minutes. Cut the cheese into slices and place over the meat. Return the casserole without the lid to the oven and bake until the cheese melts.

Veal Palermo

⅓ cup plain flour
⅓ cup grated Parmesan cheese
½ teaspoon salt
dash of pepper
6 veal cutlets
1 egg
oil for frying
1 large onion peeled and thinly
   sliced
1 green pepper seeded and thinly
   sliced
½ cup tomato purée or sauce
¼ cup water
2 teaspoons vinegar
1 tablespoon Worcester sauce
2 teaspoons chilli sauce
1 teaspoon prepared mustard
dash of garlic salt

Combine the flour, grated cheese, salt and pepper. Trim the veal cutlets and flatten them with a meat mallet. Dip each piece in beaten egg and then in the flour-cheese mixture. Heat the oil in a pan and brown the veal on both sides, drain and arrange in a single layer in a shallow casserole. Top with the onion slices and the green pepper slices.

Remove all the oil from the pan and add the tomato purée, water, vinegar, Worcester sauce, chilli sauce, prepared mustard and garlic salt. Bring to the boil, stirring constantly, scraping any browned bits of meat or coating from the bottom of the pan. Pour this liquid over the veal in the casserole, cover and cook in a moderate oven (325° F, 160° C) for 35 to 40 minutes.

Veal Paprika

2 lb or 1 kg boneless veal cut into
   1-inch cubes
3 tablespoons plain flour
1 teaspoon salt
dash of pepper
1 teaspoon dry mustard
3 tablespoons melted butter
2 medium onions chopped
1 clove of garlic crushed

Roll the cubes of veal in a mixture of 2 tablespoons of flour, the salt, pepper and mustard. Heat the butter in a heavy-based pan and fry the onions. Add the garlic, lift out and place in a casserole.

In the same pan fry the coated veal pieces lightly until brown (veal will not brown as well as beef or lamb). Lift out with a slotted spoon and place in the casserole.

Add a little more butter to the pan, add the

1 cup stock, or water and 1 soup
  cube or instant stock powder
1 cup tomato purée
squeeze of lemon juice
1 tablespoon paprika
½ cup button mushrooms
½ cup cultured or fresh cream
1 teaspoon chopped parsley

remaining tablespoon of flour and stir until brown. Add the stock, tomato purée and lemon juice, and stir until boiling. Pour over the veal in the casserole. Add the paprika and button mushrooms. Cover and cook in a moderate oven (350° F, 180° C) for about 1½ hours or until the veal is tender. Just before serving, pour the cream on top and sprinkle with chopped parsley.

Veal Parmigiana

1½ tablespoons butter
⅓ cup soft white breadcrumbs
1 tablespoon grated Parmesan
  cheese
½ teaspoon salt
dash of pepper
4 veal cutlets
1 egg
1 cup tomato juice
½ teapoon oregano
¼ teaspoon sugar
dash of onion salt
4 thin slices of Mozzarella cheese
lemon and parsley to garnish

Melt the butter in a flame-proof casserole or in a pan. Mix the breadcrumbs, grated cheese, salt and pepper. Dip the veal into slightly beaten egg and then into the cheese crumb mixture. Place in the dish containing the butter and bake uncovered in a hot oven (450° F, 230° C) for 20 minutes.

Combine the tomato juice, oregano, sugar, and onion salt in a saucepan and bring to the boil. Pour round the veal and top with the cheese slices. Return the casserole to the oven to bake until the cheese melts and the sauce bubbles. Serve with a lemon and parsley garnish.

Veal Rolls Divan

6 thin veal steaks
3 rashers of bacon
1 cup prepared stuffing mix
butter or margarine
oil for frying
1 packet frozen broccoli thawed
1 chicken soup cube dissolved in
  ½ cup hot water
10½ oz or 298 g can cream of
  celery soup
⅓ cup milk

Pound the veal steaks with a meat mallet to about ⅛ inch thick. Cook the bacon in a pan until crisp. Lift out and drain it, reserving the bacon fat. Prepare the stuffing according to the directions on the packet, using the bacon drippings from the pan made up to one-third of a cup with melted butter. Crumble the bacon and stir it into the stuffing.

Place about 1 tablespoon of the stuffing on each piece of veal and roll up. Secure with white string or wooden cocktail picks. Heat a little oil in a pan and brown the rolls. Arrange the thawed broccoli in the bottom of a lightly greased casserole and top with the veal rolls. Heat the stock made from the soup cube in the pan in which the veal rolls were browned, scraping any brown bits from the bottom of the pan. Pour this stock over the rolls in the casserole, cover and cook in a moderate oven (350° F, 180° C) for about 1 hour. Combine the celery soup and the milk in a saucepan and bring to the boil. Remove the string or cocktail picks from the veal rolls and pour the soup mixture over them. Return the casserole to the oven to reheat before serving.

Veal Scaloppini with Asparagus

2 lb or 1 kg trimmed veal cut into very thin slices
1½ tablespoons butter
⅓ cup sherry
⅔ cup stock, or water and 2 teaspoons instant mushroom stock
1½ tablespoons plain flour
2 teaspoons tomato paste
dash of cayenne pepper
1 small bay-leaf crushed
10 oz or 283 g can asparagus tips
¼ lb or 125 g cultivated mushrooms sliced
2 teaspoons butter (for the mushrooms)

Cut the slices of veal into thin strips. Melt the 1½ tablespoons butter in a saucepan and brown the veal in it quickly on all sides. Add the sherry, bring to the boil, then simmer for about 5 minutes. Combine the stock, flour, tomato paste, cayenne pepper and crushed bay-leaf and stir until boiling. Transfer to a lightly greased casserole. Cover and cook in a moderate oven (350° F, 180° C) for about 45 minutes, then add the well-drained asparagus and the mushrooms which have been sautéed in the 2 teaspoons butter. Cover and cook for a further 15 minutes.

White Scaloppini

6 veal cutlets thinly sliced
½ cup plain flour
1 teaspoon salt
pinch of pepper
3 tablespoons butter or margarine
1 tablespoon oil
1 onion peeled and chopped

Pound the veal cutlets till very thin, then coat them with a mixture of flour, salt and pepper. Heat half the butter and the oil in a heavy-based pan and brown the meat quickly on all sides. Lift out and place in a lightly greased casserole.

Add the remaining butter to the pan and sauté the chopped onion, sliced mushroom and crushed garlic for 5 minutes. Add the wine, stock, lemon

½ lb or 250 g mushrooms sliced
2 cloves of garlic crushed
1 cup dry white wine
½ cup chicken stock
2 teaspoons lemon juice
½ teaspoon thyme
2 tablespoons plain flour
3 tablespoons cold water
½ cup cultured sour cream

juice and thyme and bring to the boil. Pour over the veal in the casserole, cover and cook in a moderate oven (350° F, 180° C) for about 1 hour or until the meat is tender.

Blend the flour to a smooth paste with the cold water. Remove the casserole from the oven, stir in the blended mixture, cover and replace in the oven to cook for a further 15 minutes. Add the sour cream and reheat thoroughly.

VEGETABLES

Asparagus Casserole

15½ oz or 439 g can asparagus
  spears
3 eggs
1 teaspoon salt
¼ teaspoon pepper
¾ cup soft white breadcrumbs
1 green pepper seeded and finely
  chopped
1 cup packaged cheese cut into
  ½-inch cubes
1 cup milk
1½ tablespoons butter
tomato slices and parsley to
  garnish

Drain the asparagus well and cut it into 2-inch pieces and place in a lightly greased shallow casserole or tart plate. Beat the eggs until well mixed, then add the salt, pepper, breadcrumbs, green pepper, cheese cubes and milk. Pour over the asparagus. Melt the butter and pour over the top, then bake without the lid in a moderate oven (350° F, 180° C) for 30 or 40 minutes or until the custard mixture has set. Serve garnished with tomato slices and parsley.

Asparagus Savoury

15½ oz or 439 g can asparagus
  spears
4 hard-boiled eggs shelled and
  sliced
2 cups sliced cooked potatoes
2 rashers crisply cooked bacon
3 teaspoons butter
1½ tablespoons plain flour
¼ teaspoon salt
pinch of pepper
1½ cups milk
¼ cup grated cheese
2 tablespoons buttered
  breadcrumbs

Drain the asparagus spears and cut them into 2-inch lengths. Place in a lightly greased casserole and top with a layer of sliced eggs, then with a layer of potato slices. Add the crumbled bacon.

Make a white sauce by melting the butter in a small saucepan, adding the flour and stirring until smooth. Cook for 1 minute without browning, then season with the salt and pepper, add the milk and stir until the sauce boils and thickens. Simmer for 3 minutes. Pour over the ingredients in the casserole and sprinkle with the grated cheese and the buttered breadcrumbs. Bake uncovered at 350° F (180° C) for about 20 minutes or until the crumbs brown, the

parsley sprigs to garnish

cheese melts and the sauce bubbles. Garnish with parsley before serving.

Brain and Vegetable Casserole

1 large onion
3 small carrots
4 stalks celery
4 rashers of bacon diced
1½ tablespoons butter
1 bay-leaf
1 tablespoon minced parsley
pinch of thyme
6 sets cooked brains
1 cup cream of chicken soup
¼ cup white wine

Finely chop the onion, carrot and celery, and place in a frying pan with the diced bacon (rind removed) and the butter to sauté for about 10 minutes. Add the bay-leaf, parsley and thyme.

Remove from the heat and place in a lightly greased casserole. Arrange the cooked brains on top (they may be cut into 1-inch pieces or each set of brains may be divided in half). Mix the chicken soup with the wine and pour over the contents of the casserole. Cover and cook in a moderate oven (350° F, 180° C) for about 30 minutes.

Creole Cabbage Rolls

1 cabbage (about 4 lb or 2 kg)
1 lb or 500 g minced steak
1 cup cooked rice
¾ cup chopped onion
¼ cup chopped parsley
salt and pepper
few drops hot pepper sauce
1 egg
1 clove of garlic, crushed
¼ cup chopped green pepper
2 tablespoons butter
15 oz or 425 g can tomato soup
1 beef soup cube
¼ cup lemon juice

Pull off and discard the outside leaves of the cabbage, then rinse the firm head in cold running water. Turn it upside down and cut out the core with a sharp knife, making the incision about 3 inches deep. Place the cabbage in a large saucepan of boiling, slightly salted water and as the leaves wilt remove them one at a time, using tongs. Drain on a cloth or on white kitchen paper. Cut out the coarsest part of the rib from each leaf, making the leaves ready to fill.

Combine the steak, rice, ¼ cup of the onion, and the parsley with 1 teaspoon salt, ¼ teaspoon pepper, the hot pepper sauce and the egg, mixing lightly but thoroughly. Divide evenly to cover the number of cabbage leaves you have prepared. Place some of the meat-rice mixture on each leaf and roll up, folding in the ends and securing if necessary with wooden cocktail picks. Place seam-side down in a large, lightly greased casserole.

Sauté the garlic, the remaining ½ cup of onion and the green pepper in the butter for 2 or 3 minutes, season with ½ teaspoon salt and a dash of pepper and add the tomato soup, crumbled soup cube and lemon juice. Simmer gently for 10 minutes, then spoon over the cabbage rolls. Cover and cook in a moderate oven (350° F, 180° C) for about 1 hour. Allow two rolls per serve.

Egg and Asparagus Casserole

6 hard-boiled eggs
2 tablespoons mayonnaise
seasoned salt and pepper
$\frac{1}{2}$ teaspoon curry powder
10 oz or 283 g can asparagus
2 tablespoons butter
2 slightly rounded tablespoons
  plain flour
$1\frac{1}{2}$ cups milk
$\frac{1}{2}$ cup liquid drained from the
  asparagus
1 teaspoon made mustard
$\frac{1}{2}$ cup grated cheese
$\frac{1}{2}$ cup buttered breadcrumbs

Cut each hard-boiled egg in half lengthwise and remove the yolk, keeping the white intact. Mash or sieve the yolks and add the mayonnaise, salt, pepper and curry powder. Spoon this mixture back into the egg-white cases. Arrange the well-drained asparagus in the bottom of a lightly greased casserole and top with the stuffed eggs.

Melt the butter in a small saucepan and add the flour. Stir until smooth, then cook for 2 minutes without browning. Add the milk and the asparagus liquid and cook, stirring constantly, until the sauce boils and thickens. Add the mustard and half the grated cheese. Pour this sauce over the eggs and asparagus in the casserole and top with the remaining cheese and the buttered breadcrumbs. Bake uncovered in a moderate oven (350° F, 180° C) for about 15 minutes or until the cheese melts and lightly browns, the crumbs brown and the sauce bubbles.

Ham and Asparagus Bake

2 tablespoons butter
2 tablespoons plain flour
$1\frac{1}{2}$ cups milk
dash of pepper
$\frac{1}{4}$ teaspoon dry mustard
4 oz or 125 g ham diced
$15\frac{1}{2}$ oz or 439 g can asparagus
  spears
$\frac{1}{2}$ cup buttered breadcrumbs
parsley to garnish

Melt the butter in a saucepan and add the flour. Stir until smooth, then cook for 1 minute without browning. Add the milk and stir until the sauce boils and thickens. Flavour with the pepper and mustard and simmer for 2 or 3 minutes. Fold in the ham and the well-drained asparagus spears. Turn the mixture into a greased casserole and top with the buttered breadcrumbs. Bake uncovered at 350° F (180° C) for about 30 minutes or until the crumbs have browned and the sauce is bubbly. Garnish with parsley sprigs.

Harvest Casserole

1 large onion peeled and sliced
1 clove of garlic crushed
1 tablespoon olive oil
½ small green pepper seeded and
   sliced
1 cup sliced mushrooms
15½ oz or 439 g can kernel-style
   corn
1 rounded tablespoon butter
1 rounded tablespoon plain flour
¾ cup liquid drained from the
   corn
¾ cup milk
1½ cups grated sharp cheese
½ teaspoon salt
¼ cup minced parsley
½ cup soft white breadcrumbs
½ teaspoon oregano
¼ teaspoon pepper

In a large pan sauté the onion and garlic in the oil until the onion is soft, then add the pepper and the mushrooms. Cover and cook over low heat for about 5 minutes. Drain the corn, reserving the liquid.

Melt the butter in a small saucepan and stir in the flour, cook for 1 minute, then add the corn liquid and the milk and cook over medium heat, stirring constantly, until the sauce boils and thickens. Cook for 2 minutes. Add the cheese and salt and stir until the cheese has melted.

Lightly grease a casserole and place half the corn in the bottom, add half the pepper-mushroom mixture, then half the cheese sauce. Combine the parsley, breadcrumbs, oregano and pepper in a bowl and when well mixed sprinkle half over the contents of the casserole. Repeat the layers, ending with crumb mixture. Cover and cook at 350° F (180° C) for about 30 minutes. Remove the lid and cook for another 20 minutes or until the crumbs brown.

Harvest Casserole

Layered Tomato Rice Casserole

1 lb or 500 g finely minced steak
¼ cup chopped onion
½ cup soft white breadcrumbs
¼ cup chopped green pepper
pinch of pepper
1¼ cups undiluted tomato soup
3 cups cooked rice
½ cup grated cheese
parsley sprigs to garnish

Mix the minced steak with the onion, breadcrumbs, green pepper, pepper and ½ cup of the undiluted tomato soup. Place in a saucepan and stir over medium heat until the meat changes colour. Cover and cook, stirring frequently, for about 10 or 15 minutes.

Mix together the cooked rice, the remaining ¾ cup of undiluted tomato soup and the grated cheese. Spread half of this rice mixture in the bottom of a lightly greased casserole, add the meat mixture, then top with the remainder of the rice mixture. Bake uncovered in a moderate oven (350° F, 180° C) for 15 to 20 minutes. Serve with a parsley garnish.

Mushroom Casserole

½ lb or 250 g fresh mushrooms
3 tablespoons butter
2 sets brains
3 tablespoons seasoned plain flour
1 medium onion or ½ bunch
  shallots finely chopped
¼ cup (about 2 tablespoons)
  chopped ham
1 cup stock
1 dessertspoon Vermouth
1 or 2 tomatoes sliced
breadcrumbs

Wash, drain and slice the mushrooms, reserving a few for garnishing. Melt 1 tablespoon of the butter in a pan and sauté the mushrooms until tender. Drain, reserving the liquid, and place the mushrooms in the bottom of a lightly greased casserole.

To cook the brains, first soak for 30 minutes in cold water. Drain and remove the fine skin, place the brains in a saucepan, cover with cold water and bring to the boil. Drain off this water, add fresh cold water with a little salt, and if liked, a bay-leaf, bring to the boil and simmer for 10 minutes. Drain.

Toss the cooked brains in seasoned flour, add 1 tablespoon butter to the pan used for the mushrooms and brown the brains on all sides. Lift out and place in the casserole.

Add the remaining tablespoon of butter to the pan and sauté the chopped onion, then stir in the chopped ham. Lift out with a slotted spoon and distribute over the brains in the casserole.

Add the remaining flour to the pan, stir until it browns, add the stock, the Vermouth and the liquid drained from the mushrooms. Cook, stirring constantly, until the mixture boils and thickens. Pour over the contents of the casserole. Top with tomato slices and the reserved mushrooms, sprinkle with breadcrumbs and bake uncovered in a moderate oven (350° F, 180° C) or place under the griller to cook the tomatoes and brown the breadcrumbs.

Potato and Mushroom Casserole

1 lb or 500 g new potatoes
½ lb or 250 g button mushrooms
2 tablespoons butter
2 tablespoons plain flour
1 cup milk
1 cup potato water
2 tablespoons cream
pinch of grated nutmeg

Wash the potatoes and cook them whole in boiling salted water. Drain and reserve 1 cup of the cooking liquid. Return the potatoes to the saucepan in which they were cooked, cover and steam for about 5 minutes, then remove the skins.

Wipe the mushrooms—do not peel if they are the cultivated variety. Heat half the butter in a small saucepan, add the mushrooms and sauté for about 5 minutes. Lift out with a slotted spoon.

Put the remainder of the butter into the saucepan, add the flour and stir until smooth, then cook for 1 minute without browning. Add the milk and potato liquid (or all milk if you like) and stir until the sauce boils and thickens. Place the cooked potatoes (whole if they are small, but thickly sliced if they are large) with the sautéed mushrooms in a lightly greased casserole. Add the cream and nutmeg to the sauce and pour over the contents of the casserole, cover and cook in a moderate oven (350° F, 180° C) for about 15 minutes.

Potato and Onion Casserole

6 potatoes peeled and coarsely
   chopped
3 medium onions peeled and
   chopped
2 teaspoons chopped parsley

Mix the potatoes, onions, parsley and celery leaves and season with the thyme, marjoram, salt and pepper. Place in a lightly greased casserole dish and dot the top with butter. Cook in a moderate oven (350° F, 180° C) for about 45

1 tablespoon chopped celery
    leaves
good pinch of thyme
good pinch of marjoram
1 teaspoon salt
¼ teaspoon pepper
1 tablespoon butter

minutes, removing the lid after 20 minutes to brown the top.

Potato Aubergine Scallop

1 lb or 500 g medium potatoes
1 aubergine (about 4 oz or 125 g)
lemon juice
salt
freshly ground pepper
4 oz or 125 g butter
½ medium onion peeled and
    sliced
½ medium green pepper cut into
    strips
1 tablespoon chopped parsley

Peel the potatoes and boil them in salted water until soft in the centres. Drain, cool and cut into ⅛-inch slices. Slice the aubergine finely and toss in lemon juice. Alternate the potato slices with the aubergine slices in a lightly greased shallow casserole, seasoning each layer with salt and pepper.

Melt the butter in a pan, sauté the onion and pepper for 3 to 4 minutes, then toss in the parsley. Spoon this mixture over the potatoes and aubergines. Cover and cook in a moderate oven (350° F, 180° C) for 20 to 25 minutes.

Potato Moussaka

1 large onion peeled and diced
1 tablespoon oil
1 clove of garlic crushed
1 lb or 500 g ground steak
1 teaspoon salt
¼ teaspoon pepper
1 tablespoon minced parsley
1 teaspoon chopped mint
pinch of cinnamon
½ bay-leaf crumbled
4 cups thinly sliced peeled
    potatoes
¼ cup tomato paste
1 cup water
1 beef soup cube
For the cream topping
2 teaspoons plain flour

Cook the onion in the heated oil until soft. Add the garlic and the minced steak. Cook, stirring until lightly browned. Add the salt, pepper, parsley, mint, cinnamon and crumbled bay-leaf. Cook for 5 minutes. Layer this meat mixture in a lightly greased casserole with the sliced potatoes, seasoning each layer with salt, and ending with potatoes.

Mix the tomato paste with ¼ cup water and stir into the pan in which the meat was browned. Add the remaining water and the soup cube and bring to the boil. Pour over the contents of the casserole. Cover and cook in a moderate oven (350° F, 180° C) for about 30 minutes or until most of the liquid has been absorbed and the potatoes are nearly tender.

Remove the casserole from the oven. For the

1 cup cream
2 egg yolks
¼ cup grated Parmesan cheese

cream topping combine the flour, cream and well-beaten egg yolks and pour it over the contents of the casserole. Sprinkle with the grated Parmesan cheese. Replace in the oven and bake uncovered for a further 15 or 20 minutes or until the custard topping has set and is golden.

Scalloped Corn and Tomatoes

3 rashers of bacon
2 cups thinly sliced onion
¼ cup diced green pepper
1 cup packaged stuffing mix
1 cup canned cream-style corn
3½ cups stewed tomatoes
½ teaspoon salt
2 teaspoons sugar
dash of pepper
pinch of thyme
pinch of marjoram
pinch of oregano
2 teaspoons butter melted
parsley sprigs to garnish

Remove the rind and fry the bacon until crisp. Remove from the pan and set aside. Sauté the onion slices and the green pepper in a little butter or fat until tender. Add the stuffing mix, corn and tomatoes. Flavour with the salt, sugar, pepper, thyme, marjoram and oregano, then crumble the bacon and add it to the mixture with the melted butter. Turn the mixture into a greased casserole or into individual ramekins and bake uncovered in a moderate oven (350° F, 180° C) for about 30 minutes. Serve garnished with parsley.

Scalloped Potatoes

6 large potatoes
4 rashers of bacon
1½ teaspoons salt
⅜ teaspoon garlic salt
⅜ teaspoon paprika
1 tablespoon chopped parsley
1 cup chopped shallots including
    some of the green tops
1 cup chopped celery
1 cup grated cheese
1½ tablespoons butter
⅔ cup milk

Peel the potatoes and cut them into ⅛-inch-thick slices. You will need about 6 cups in all. Cover with iced water and allow to stand while you prepare the other ingredients.

Fry the bacon until crisp, drain on crumpled paper and when cool enough to handle crumble in the fingers. Grease a large casserole with butter and cover the bottom with a layer of potatoes which have been well drained. Use about 2 cups at this stage. Now sprinkle evenly with ½ teaspoon salt, ⅛ teaspoon garlic salt, ⅛ teaspoon paprika, 1 teaspoon parsley, half the crumbled bacon, half the shallots, half the celery and half the cheese. Dot with butter.

Add another layer of potatoes and repeat all the layers in the order listed. Finish with a layer

Scalloped Potatoes

of potatoes. Pour the milk over the top and bake uncovered in a hot oven (400° F, 200° C) for 30 minutes, then reduce the heat to 350° F (180° C) and continue baking for another 20 to 30 minutes or until the potatoes are tender and the top layer is a golden brown.

Spanish Corn Casserole

15 oz or 425 g can peeled
   tomatoes
15 oz or 425 g can whole kernel-
   style corn
$\frac{1}{2}$ cup finely chopped green pepper
$\frac{1}{2}$ cup finely chopped onion
$\frac{3}{4}$ teaspoon salt
dash of pepper
$\frac{1}{2}$ cup soft white breadcrumbs
1 tablespoon butter melted

Combine the tomatoes with the well-drained corn, the green pepper, onion, salt and pepper. Toss the breadcrumbs in the melted butter and sprinkle over the ingredients in a lightly greased casserole. Bake uncovered in a moderate oven (350° F, 180° C) for 30 minutes.

Stuffed Cabbage Rolls

2 small onions peeled and
   chopped
1 tablespoon oil
1 lb or 500 g finely minced steak
½ teaspoon mixed herbs
1 soup cube
salt and pepper
½ cup cooked rice
1 medium cabbage
10½ oz or 298 g can tomato soup
4 tablespoons water
2 teaspoons vinegar
2 teaspoons lemon juice
1 teaspoon sugar
⅔ cup cultured sour cream or
   thick fresh cream
paprika

Fry the onion in the oil. Add the minced steak, herbs, soup cube, salt and pepper. Cook, stirring constantly, for about 5 minutes. Remove from the heat and add the rice.

Take the large leaves off the cabbage and soften them by cooking for 2 or 3 minutes in boiling salted water. Drain, then cut away the thick stem ends of the leaves. Place 1 tablespoon of the meat and rice mixture on each cabbage leaf and roll up. Secure each roll with a wooden cocktail pick. Pack neatly and tightly in a lightly greased casserole dish.

Combine the soup, water, vinegar, lemon juice and sugar and pour over the rolls. Cover and cook in a moderate oven (350° F, 180° C) for about 1 hour. When ready to serve, pour over the cream and sprinkle with the paprika.

Tomato, Celery and Mushroom Medley

½ lb or 250 g celery cut into
   2-inch diagonal spears
1 oz or 30 g butter
½ lb or 250 g small firm
   cultivated mushrooms
½ lb or 250 g ripe tomatoes
   quartered
½ cup tomato purée
1 tablespoon lemon juice
salt and pepper
2 oz or 60 g grated matured
   Australian Cheddar cheese

Boil the celery in salted water for 5 to 7 minutes. Drain, then rinse in cold water. Melt the butter in a pan, add the mushrooms and sauté gently until all are coated with butter. Add the celery, tomato quarters, tomato purée and lemon juice. Season to taste with salt and freshly ground black pepper. Place in a lightly greased casserole, cover and cook in a moderate oven (350° F, 180° C) for 20 minutes. Uncover, sprinkle with the cheese, then return the casserole to the oven for a further 10 minutes or until the cheese melts.

Tomato Cheese Custard

1 lb 12 oz or 794 g can peeled
   tomatoes
1 teaspoon instant minced onion
2 teaspoons butter
1½ teaspoons salt

Combine the first five ingredients in a saucepan and stir over medium heat for about 15 minutes. Stir in the breadcrumbs and allow to cool. Add the eggs and stir to blend evenly, then pour into a lightly greased medium-sized casserole. Top

¼ teaspoon pepper
¾ cup soft white breadcrumbs
2 slightly beaten eggs
½ cup grated Cheddar cheese
sliced stuffed olives to garnish

with the cheese, set the casserole in a dish containing hot water and bake uncovered at 375° F (190° C) for about 40 minutes or until set. Garnish with sliced stuffed olives and serve warm.

Tomato Egg Casserole

2 tablespoons butter
1½ tablespoons plain flour
1½ cups milk
salt and pepper
½ cup grated Cheddar cheese
6 hard-boiled eggs shelled and
   sliced
3 large tomatoes peeled and
   thickly sliced
3 cooked carrots cut into slices
¼ cup buttered breadcrumbs

Melt 1½ tablespoons of the butter in a saucepan and add the flour. Stir until smooth, cook for 1 minute without browning, then add the milk. Cook, stirring constantly, until the sauce boils and thickens, cook for a further 2 minutes, then season to taste with salt and pepper and stir in the cheese.

Place half the egg slices in the bottom of a lightly greased casserole, reserve 6 tomato slices for topping and put the remainder in a layer over the eggs. Spoon over some of the sauce. Add the carrot slices and the remaining eggs and pour over the remainder of the sauce.

Sprinkle the buttered breadcrumbs round the edge of the dish and arrange the reserved tomato slices on top. Dot the tomatoes with the remaining butter, cover and cook in a moderate oven (350° F, 180° C) for about 30 minutes.

Vegetable Casserole

4 rashers of bacon coarsely
   chopped
½ lb or 250 g mushrooms
   quartered
1 clove of garlic crushed or
   minced
good pinch of dried basil
10½ oz or 298 g can cream of
   chicken soup
dash of pepper
1½ cups diagonally sliced celery
2 cups diagonally sliced carrot
8 tiny white onions peeled
3 small turnips peeled and cubed

Sauté the chopped bacon in a heavy-based saucepan until the fat is clear, then lift out with a slotted spoon. Cook the mushrooms in the bacon fat left in the saucepan. Add the garlic, the basil and the soup, season with pepper and set aside.

Place the sliced celery and carrot and the onions and cubed turnips in boiling salted water, cover, bring to the boil and cook for 10 minutes. Drain well.

Arrange the zucchini halves in a single layer in the bottom of a lightly greased casserole, top with the other vegetables, then pour in the soup mixture. Cover and cook at 350° F (180° C) for

4 small zucchini halved lengthwise
lemon juice
chopped parsley to garnish

about 1 hour. Stir in some lemon juice according to taste, and garnish with chopped parsley and the reserved bacon.

Vegetable Medley

2½ teaspoons salt
2 teaspoons sugar
½ teaspoon mixed herbs
dash of pepper
1 cup diagonally cut celery
1½ cups sliced green beans
2 cups diagonally sliced carrots
3 medium tomatoes peeled and
  sliced
1 green pepper seeded and cut
  into rings
1 onion peeled and sliced
¼ cup butter

Combine the salt, sugar, mixed herbs and pepper. In an ungreased casserole arrange half the celery, beans, carrot and tomato slices, green pepper rings and sliced onion. Sprinkle with half the mixed herbs and dot with half the butter. Repeat, using the remaining vegetables, mixed herbs and butter. Cover and cook in a moderate oven (350° F, 180° C) for about 1 hour, stirring occasionally.